HOLT McDOUGAL LITERATURE

Resource Manager

Unit 1

GRADE 8

HOLT McDOUGAL
a division of Houghton Mifflin Harcourt

ISBN-13 978-0-547-61868-5

4 5 6 7 8 9 10   .1409   18 17 16 15 14 13 12 11
4500334521   ^ B C D E F G

Resource Manager

What Is It?

The Resource Manager brings together in one place the rich body of resources provided by *Holt McDougal Literature*. These are some of the tools you'll find here:

Beginning the year

- an overview of program components
- planning for differentiated instruction
- resources for creating a classroom profile
- options for instructional paths
- thematic opportunities for teaching the selections

Teaching a unit

- tools for grammar instruction
- academic vocabulary for English learners

Teaching a selection

For you, the teacher

- lesson plan and resource guide
- leveled selection questions
- ideas for extension
- answer keys

For your students

- copy masters customized to teach and reinforce the focus standards in each selection and workshop
- copy masters to preteach and reinforce vocabulary
- reading fluency copy masters

Resource Manager Pages

The selections and workshops in the anthology are supported by the following types of Resource Manager pages.

SELECTION AND WORKSHOP RESOURCES

Teacher Planning Pages
Lesson at a Glance
Lesson Plan and Resource Guide
Additional Selection Questions
Ideas for Extension
Teacher Notes

Student Copy Masters with Selections
Summary (translations in Spanish, Haitian Creole, Vietnamese)
Text Analysis
Reading Skill
Vocabulary Study
Vocabulary Practice
Vocabulary Strategy
Reading Check
Question Support
Grammar in Context
Reading Fluency

Student Copy Masters with Workshops
Unit Introduction
Academic Vocabulary
Text Analysis Workshop
Note Taking
Media Study
Viewing Guide Summary
Close Viewing
Media Activity
Production Template
Writing Workshop
Planning / Prewriting
Drafting
Revising and Editing
Ask a Peer Reader
Scoring Rubric
Speaking and Listening
Technology Workshop
Writing Support (for English language learners)

A Sampler of Resource Manager Pages

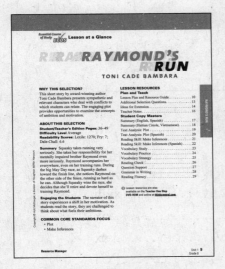

The **Lesson at a Glance,** a teacher planning page, outlines the lesson. It includes a summary and readability scores for each selection.

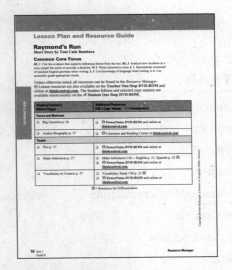

The **Lesson Plan and Resource Guide** suggests a step-by-step plan for teaching a lesson, along with the program resources to use at each step.

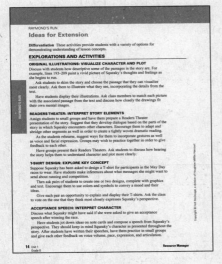

The Ideas for Extension feature offers a variety of ways to enrich and extend the lesson concepts through activities, research, and writing.

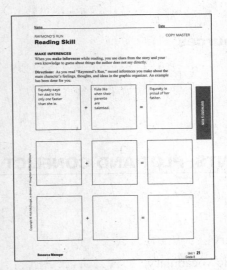

A **Reading Skill** copy master contains the graphic organizer introduced in the Student's Edition. Students use the organizer to track the focus skill while reading a selection.

Table of Contents

UNIT 2
THROUGH DIFFERENT EYES: CHARACTER AND POINT OF VIEW

Contents

Unit Planning

Selection and Workshop Resources

UNIT 3
THE PLACE TO BE: SETTING AND MOOD

Contents

UNIT 4
A WORLD OF MEANING: THEME AND SYMBOL

Contents

UNIT 5
PAINTING WITH WORDS: POETRY

UNIT 6
A UNIQUE IMPRINT: STYLE, VOICE, AND TONE

UNIT 7
OUR PLACE IN THE WORLD: HISTORY, CULTURE, AND THE AUTHOR

UNIT 8
BELIEVE IT OR NOT: FACTS AND INFORMATION

Contents 1

Unit Planning

Selection and Workshop Resources

UNIT 9
STATE YOUR CASE: ARGUMENT AND PERSUASION

Contents 1

Unit Planning

UNIT 10
THE POWER OF RESEARCH

Contents

Unit Planning

Workshop Resources

The Program at a Glance

Teacher Resources

Time-saving, easy-to-use teacher resources make lesson planning and preparation simple.

Core Teacher Resources include:

Teacher's Edition

Teacher One Stop DVD-ROM with ExamView Test Generator

Resource Manager

MediaSmart DVD-ROM
Helps promote critical thinking through analysis of a variety of media

WriteSmart CD-ROM
An interactive writing-instruction tool with a rubric generator

PowerNotes DVD-ROM
Highly visual PowerPoint presentations and motivational video trailers introduce key lessons in the Student Edition.

ThinkCentral Online Assessment
- Diagnostic and Selection Tests
- Unit and Benchmark Tests
- Level Up Online Tutorials for Remediation

Assessment File
Provides comprehensive opportunities to assess student progress with an array of tests.

Best Practices Toolkit
Motivate students with engaging activities and over 200 graphic organizer transparencies.

Professional Development for Language Arts DVD
Features video interviews with leading experts in differentiation, vocabulary reading comprehension, and more.

Student Resources

A complete program of technology and print resources provides support for differentiated student learning.

Core Student Resources include:

Student Edition

Student One Stop DVD-ROM

Interactive Reader

Adapted Interactive Reader

English Language Learner Adapted Interactive Reader

Adapted Interactive Reader: Audio Tutor

Audio Anthology
Enables students to hear pronunciation, phrasing, and interpretations as they follow along in their textbook.

thinkcentral.com
Provides access to the online version of the Student Edition, as well as a wealth of interactive resources, video trailers, and audio support.

Novels
Many novels, works of nonfiction, and plays promote independent learning and reading.

Language Handbook
Supports systematic, student-friendly instruction in all aspects of grammar, usage, and mechanics.

Planning for Differentiated Instruction

The students in your classroom span the spectrum of academic readiness, cultural diversity, personal interests, and learning styles. A key philosophy of this program is to give you the tools you need to teach *all* of your students. These three steps will help you differentiate instruction using *Holt McDougal Literature:*

STEP 1: Get to know your students.	STEP 2: Identify your resources.	STEP 3: Choose your lesson options.
The strategies below, along with the student copy masters that follow, will help you create a classroom profile.	Use page xviii to get capsule descriptions of program resources for adapting instruction.	Use page xix to view four different instructional paths.

Step 1. Get to Know Your Students

Creating and Using a Classroom Profile

What is the unique make-up of your classroom? A good first step in diversifying instruction is creating a classroom profile—in other words, getting to know your students' individual abilities, interests, and experiences. For example, you might want to know the following things about each of your students:

• reading level
• proficiency with key content vocabulary
• how they feel about themselves as students
• what they enjoy doing when not in school
• how they feel about school in general

Use the assessment components of *Holt McDougal Literature* to obtain data about students' skill level and academic readiness. In addition, the students themselves can provide you with important information. Use the copy masters that follow—a **student profile** and an **interest inventory**—to gather students' insights into their own needs.

As you collect the pertinent information, a unique classroom profile will emerge. Use this information, along with the program's differentiation resources, to create personalized instruction. For example, you may want to

• ensure access to advanced materials for students whose work is consistently strong
• scaffold instruction for those who need more help
• plan small group work that takes student interests, abilities, or work styles into account
• tap student motivation through writing prompts or activities built around topics of high student interest

Student Profile Survey

Directions These phrases describe ways that some people learn and what their preferences are. Write the phrases that best fit you in the "This Best Describes Me" column. Place the phrases that don't fit you in the "This Is Not Like Me" column. It isn't necessary to use all the phrases. Leave out the ones you are unsure about.

- Very logical
- Move around when I learn
- Great at planning
- Comfortable in the spotlight
- Sit still when I learn
- Very creative
- Prefer quiet when I work
- Like to do several things at a time
- Enjoy working with words
- Like art
- Prefer to work alone
- Not great at planning
- Enjoy working with ideas

- Prefer noise and activity when I work
- Enjoy working with numbers
- Like music
- Enjoy working with objects
- Prefer to be in the background
- Like science
- Prefer to decide on my own what to do
- Like collecting things
- Prefer to do one thing at a time
- Like the outdoors
- Prefer to work with people
- Like making things
- Prefer to be told how to do things

This Best Describes Me	This Is Not Like Me

In the "This Best Describes Me" column, add your own words that describe you, your interests, and your ways of learning.

Student Interest Inventory

Directions Give as much information as you can. It will help your teacher get to know you better.

1. What are your favorite interests outside of school? What do you enjoy about them?

2. What would others say are your strengths or talents?

3. What are some things you'd like to learn about? This can be in any school subject, or outside of school altogether.

4. What's difficult for you at school? This can be in a particular subject area or connected to something else entirely. What makes it hard?

5. What are you expert in?

6. What's your favorite

• book _____

• kind of music _____

• sport _____

• TV show _____

• movie _____

• video game _____

• radio station _____

7. Students use different methods to help them learn—like flashcards, memory devices, highlighting. What are some ways of learning that work for you?

8. What are some ways of learning that don't work well for you? Why?

9. In what areas would you like to improve? Why?

10. What else should I know about you as a person and a student that could help me teach you?

Step 2: Identify Your Resources for Differentiation

McDougal Littell Literature provides a wide range of resources, highlighted below, to adapt instruction for your diverse classroom. In addition to activities that support individual learning behaviors, the program supplies comprehensive support for these three groups of learners:

- students learning English
- less-proficient readers and writers
- advanced learners

AUDIO ANTHOLOGY

Professional recordings of the selections provide extra support to less-proficient readers, students learning English, and auditory learners.

RESOURCE MANAGER

A variety of copy masters help you enhance and differentiate instruction. These include

- leveled comprehension questions
- translations into Spanish, Haitian Creole, and Vietnamese
- ideas for extension
- academic vocabulary practice
- writing support

INTERACTIVE READER AND WRITER

The *InterActive Reader & Writer* is a consumable work text that pairs core selections from the main anthology with one or two high-interest nonfiction readings. Engaging students at their level, the *InterActive Reader & Writer* is a differentiated alternative to the anthology, including test-taking practice and practical tips for answering test questions.

TEACHER'S EDITION

Comprehensive support for differentiation in the teacher's edition includes

- Targeted Passages—boxed passages of key parts of a selection for less-proficient readers and English learners
- Discussion Prompts—leveled questions for group discussion of key passages
- Teacher Notes—instructional strategies and activities for the guided reading of diverse learners

BEST PRACTICES TOOLKIT

The *Best Practices Toolkit* is a valuable collection of teacher tools, mini-lessons, copy masters, and transparencies that help you differentiate instruction. Included are articles and tips by program consultants that provide a rich source of teaching ideas and methodologies to enhance lessons in a diverse classroom.

WRITING WORKSHOPS

Highly visual and engaging, the *Writing Workshops* in the student's edition provide step-by-step modeling of the writing process.

3. Choose Your Lesson Options

You can teach a selection as presented in the anthology, or you may adapt the lesson flow as follows.

PATH 1—BEGIN WITH THE BIG QUESTION (ANTHOLOGY)

Discuss the Big Question ▸ Teach the Common Core Standards Focus ▸ Read the selection, discussing the sidebar annotations ▸ Discuss the selection and postreading questions; practice vocabulary and writing ▸ Assess and reteach, or extend

PATH 2—READ BEFORE TEACHING

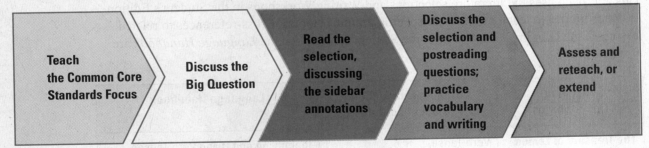

Discuss the Big Question ▸ Read the selection without looking at the sidebar annotations ▸ Teach the Common Core Standards Focus and revisit the sidebar annotations ▸ Discuss the selection and postreading questions; practice vocabulary and writing ▸ Assess and reteach, or extend

PATH 3—BEGIN WITH THE COMMON CORE STANDARDS FOCUS

Teach the Common Core Standards Focus ▸ Discuss the Big Question ▸ Read the selection, discussing the sidebar annotations ▸ Discuss the selection and postreading questions; practice vocabulary and writing ▸ Assess and reteach, or extend

PATH 4—READ AND DISCUSS

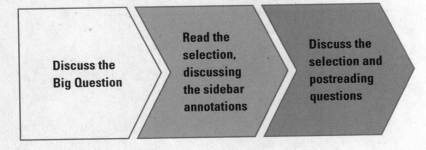

Discuss the Big Question ▸ Read the selection, discussing the sidebar annotations ▸ Discuss the selection and postreading questions

Integrating Grammar Instruction

Grammar Focus charts, provided in each unit of the *Resource Manager,* offer two methods of incorporating grammar instruction into your literature class. You may choose one approach or blend the two.

- *Systematic Grammar Instruction:* a framework for a year's worth of grammar instruction, based primarily on lessons in the *Language Handbook*
- *Integrated Grammar, Literature, and Writing:* opportunities for reinforcement and application of grammar concepts using the literature selections and Writing Workshops in the Student's Edition

Systematic Grammar Instruction

The Systematic Grammar Instruction chart, a portion of which is shown below, serves as a pacing guide and provides references to all of the grammar resources of *Holt McDougal Literature.*

Week	Grammar Handbook (Student Edition)	Language Handbook
6 Personal Pronouns	Personal Pronouns, p. R52	Identifying and Using Pronouns in the Nominative Case, p. 46

Integrated Grammar, Literature, and Writing

This approach uses the literature selections and Writing Workshops in the Student's Edition as opportunities to teach or reinforce specific grammar topics. Cross-references to related lessons in the Grammar Handbook in the Student Edition and the *Language Handbook* are also provided.

Teaching Opportunities	Grammar Handbook (Student Edition)	Language Handbook
The Treasure of Lemon Brown Use Correct Verb Tense	Verb Tense, p. R56	Identifying and Using Verb Tenses, pp. 32–33; Using Consistent Verb Tense, pp. 34–36

Thematic Opportunities

If you prefer to group your lessons by themes instead of skills, choose from the thematic opportunities on the following six pages.

Things of Value	
Big Question	**What do you value in life?** Family, friends, fame, fortune, freedom—what you value reflects the kind of person you are. What makes something valuable in your eyes? The selections in this grouping will open your eyes to the things people value.
Selections in the Anthology	• **"Clean Sweep,"** short story by Joan Bauer, pp. 66–79 While cleaning Mrs. Leonardo's attic, Katie helps the older woman discover something of real worth. • **"The Treasure of Lemon Brown,"** short story by Walter Dean Myers, pp. 176–189 When Jesse meets an old blues musician who is down on his luck, the boy gains an understanding of what is truly valuable. • **"The Old Grandfather and His Little Grandson,"** Russian folk tale by Leo Tolstoy; **"The Wise Old Woman,"** Japanese folk tale by Yoshiko Uchida, pp. 486–499 These tales make a case for holding elders in high esteem. • **"It's all I have to bring today—,"** poem by Emily Dickinson; **"We Alone,"** poem by Alice Walker; pp. 624–631 The speakers in these poems make it clear that great value can be found in everyday things. • **"The Snapping Turtle,"** short story by Joseph Bruchac, pp. 788–803 In this story about passing on traditions and values, a Native American boy must decide a turtle's true value.
Related Novels and Longer Works	***The Gospel According to Larry,*** novel by Janet Tashjian Shy, brainy Josh creates a Web site and a persona named Larry in hope of changing society's values. As "Larry" gains popularity, Josh's risk of exposure and embarrassment escalates. ***An Inconvenient Truth,*** (adapted) nonfiction by Al Gore This adapted version of Al Gore's best-selling book is a call to action to stop global warming and preserve our home, the Earth.
Wrap-Up	To assess understanding, have students respond to one of these culminating options. 1. Write a personal response to one of the selections you read. Include a summary of the selection and your thoughts about it. 2. Think of something you consider highly valuable, and brainstorm a list of memories you have about how you came to value and appreciate it. Compare your experience to those portrayed in the selections you read. 3. Choose two of the selections and use a Venn diagram to compare and contrast the role *value* plays in each. Consider what the characters or speakers find valuable, any lessons or themes about *value*, and the specific words or actions of the characters.

THEMATIC OPPORTUNITIES

	Taking a Stand	
Big Question	**When is compromise wrong?**	
	While there is great value in compromise, sometimes you have to take a stand for what you believe to be right or just. What would you risk for something you believed in? What would it take for you to commit to a cause? The selections in this grouping explore what it means to live your beliefs and take a stand.	
Selections in the Anthology	• **"Paul Revere's Ride,"** narrative poem by Henry Wadsworth Longfellow, pp. 136–143 Paul Revere takes a midnight ride to warn his countrymen of a British attack. • ***Harriet Tubman: Conductor on the Underground Railroad,*** biography by Ann Petry, pp. 266–281 Harriet Tubman risks her life and the lives of those who followed her to freedom in order to protest the evils of slavery. • **"Hallucinations,"** science fiction by Isaac Asimov, pp. 344–369 As humans begin to colonize a distant planet, a young trainee's "hallucinations" reveal that the humans are not alone. • **"the lesson of the moth,"** poem by Don Marquis; **"Identity,"** poem by Julio Noboa; pp. 616–623 Two speakers explain their philosophy of living fully. • **"I Want to Write"** and **"Sit-Ins,"** poetry by Margaret Walker, pp. 856–860 How can you fight injustice? These poems focus on the idea of working for what you believe is right.	
Related Novels and Longer Works	***Crooked River,*** historical fiction by Shelley Pearsall Rebecca knows that Indian John is innocent of murder. Will she do what is necessary to save the man's life? This novel is based on a trial that took place in Ohio in 1812. ***Last Shot,*** mystery-detective novel by John Feinstein Two young reporters win the chance to cover the NCAA Final Four basketball tournament. When they overhear a plot to "fix" the game, they have to work fast to stop the crime. ***Left for Dead: A Young Man's Search for Justice for the U.S.S. Indianapolis,*** nonfiction by Pete Nelson A school project leads to the truth about the sinking of the *U.S.S. Indianapolis,* the navy cover-up, and the captain's trial.	
Wrap-Up	To assess understanding, have students respond to one of these culminating options. 1. Take part in a debate over whether it is right to disobey an unjust law, as Harriet Tubman or the sit-in protesters did. Use details from the selection to support either side. 2. Using text and images from print sources and the Web, create a museum display honoring people who have famously taken a stand. Incorporate relevant quotations from the selections into your displays. 3. Suppose the characters and speakers from these selections were to meet at a party or awards ceremony. Write a dialogue for one of the conversations they might have regarding their beliefs or the importance of defending one's beliefs.	

Unexpected Consequences	
Big Question	**What happens when things don't go as planned?** Life can be unpredictable, so it's important to simply take things as they come. But sometimes, even the best plans have results we could never have predicted—not even in our wildest dreams. The selections in this grouping focus on what happens when things don't go according to plan.
Selections in the Anthology	• **"The Ransom of Red Chief,"** short story by O. Henry, pp. 50–65 When two thieves kidnap a child for ransom money, they get more than they asked for. • **"The Tell-Tale Heart,"** short story by Edgar Allan Poe, pp. 80–89 A man believes he has committed the perfect murder. Now, if only he can get that thumping noise to stop. . . . • **"The Hitchhiker,"** radio play by Lucille Fletcher, pp. 90–103 A man's cross-country car trip turns into a deadly nightmare because of a hitchhiker. • **"Flowers for Algernon,"** short story by Daniel Keyes pp. 196–229 Participating in an experiment may give mentally challenged Charlie the intellect he's always wanted. Why not take the risk? • **"The Monkey's Paw,"** short story by W. W. Jacobs, pp. 372–387 A man's desires lead him down a dangerous path. • **"The Lady, or the Tiger?"** short story by Frank D. Stockton pp. 704–715 In ancient times, one man's life depends on knowing the answer to "What's behind door number two?"
Related Novels and Longer Works	*Red Kayak,* novel by Priscilla Cummings Brady's world is shaken when he learns the cause of a neighbor's boating accident. *Nothing but the Truth,* documentary novel by Avi When Philip hums the national anthem during Miss Narwin's class, he sets off a series of events that soon tumble out of control. *Something Out of Nothing: Marie Curie and Radium,* biography by Carla Killough McClafferty This biography goes beyond the details of Marie Curie's life to explore the impact her discovery of radium had on the world and the negative effects it had on her life.
Wrap-Up	To assess understanding, have students respond to one of these culminating options. 1. Choose one of the selections and create a flow chart illustrating other possible consequences—intended or unintended—of the main character's actions. 2. Write a cause-and-effect essay explaining the ways in which a situation, taken from one of the selections, gets out of control. 3. Analyze the selections and, as a group, brainstorm actions the characters could have taken to avoid unintended consequences. Choose one selection and collaborate to rewrite it. In your rewrite, the characters should follow one of the alternate paths to experience a new outcome.

THEMATIC OPPORTUNITIES

	Fitting In
Big Question	**How important is it to fit in?** Everyone likes to feel accepted. But sometimes a choice has to be made between becoming what others want you to be, or being true to yourself. How do you know where you truly belong? The selections in this grouping explore what it means to find one's place.
Selections in the Anthology	• **"Going Where I'm Coming From,"** memoir by Naomi Shihab Nye, pp. 394–409 Can a person call two places "home"? The author experiences culture shock when she moves to Jerusalem—and again when she returns to the United States one year later. • **"Us and Them,"** personal essay by David Sedaris, pp. 740–751 Who decides what's "normal"? The author recalls disliking a neighborhood family simply because they seemed so abnormal. • **"Pecos Bill,"** tall tale by Mary Pope Osborne, pp. 822–831 Being raised by coyotes hasn't exactly prepared Bill for normalcy. In this tall tale, he tries to find where he belongs. • **"The Sanctuary of School,"** essay by Lynda Barry, pp. 1014–1021 Lynda Barry recalls a time in her childhood when she felt more comfortable at school than in her own home.
Related Novels and Longer Works	***American Born Chinese,*** graphic novel by Gene Luen Yang A Chinese folk hero, an Asian American boy, and a Caucasian teen with a Chinese cousin all learn lessons about accepting who you are in this award-winning graphic novel. ***Crash,*** novel by Jerry Spinelli Crash Coogan has always bullied dweeby, peace-loving Penn Webb. But when Crash's family starts to struggle, he begins to see another side to Penn, and another way to fit into his own life. ***Homecoming,*** novel by Cynthia Voigt When Dicey Tillerman's mother abandons her children, Dicey leads her brothers and sister in search of a new home.
Wrap-Up	To assess understanding, have students respond to one of these culminating options. **1.** Create a word web for each of the main characters in these selections, showing what the idea of "belonging" or "fitting in" means to them. **2.** Choose one character or person from your reading. Create a radio or video diary that describes his or her experience with fitting in. Play your diary for your class. **3.** Suppose you had your own advice column, and a character from these selections wrote in describing his or her struggle to fit in. Write the character's letter and your reply, offering advice.

THEMATIC OPPORTUNITIES

Finding Courage	
Big Question	**What does it mean to be brave?** Ordinary people sometimes find themselves in extraordinary circumstances. When forced to draw upon an inner strength and courage that has previously not been needed, they often learn something new about themselves in the process. The selections in this grouping show that courage comes in many forms.
Selections in the Anthology	• **"The Drummer Boy of Shiloh,"** short story by Ray Bradbury, pp. 328–337 The night before his first battle in the Civil War, a young drummer boy lies awake, struggling with his fears. • *The Diary of Anne Frank,* drama by Frances Goodrich and Albert Hackett, pp. 508–567 Fearing for their lives, the Frank family is forced into hiding. Young Anne, in particular, puts on a brave face and helps to encourage the others. • **"Out of Bounds,"** short story by Beverley Naidoo, pp. 804–821 Despite his fears, wealthy young Rohan helps a lower-class boy and his mother by carrying much-needed water to their home. In return, Rohan learns that he and the other boy aren't so different after all. • **"Kabul's Singing Sensation,"** magazine article by Tim McGirk, pp. 924–933 It takes courage to find one's voice in a war-torn country. One 13-year-old boy proudly sings to encourage others.
Related Novels and Longer Works	*Ask Me No Questions,* novel by Marina Budhos Nadira's family are Muslims, living illegally in the U.S. In a post-9/11 crackdown, Nadira's father is detained, and she must take charge and save the family from deportation. *Johnny Tremain,* novel by Esther Forbes In this classic story of the American Revolution, a young apprentice overcomes personal troubles and finds his inner courage when he becomes a spy for the colonial army. *A Time for Dancing,* novel by Davida Wills Hurwin Dancers Samantha and Julie are best friends. When Julie develops cancer, their relationship is put to the test. Includes mild language that may be inappropriate for some students.
Wrap-Up	To assess understanding, have students respond to one of these culminating options. 1. Write an essay comparing and contrasting the kind of courage demonstrated in two or three of the selections you read. Use details and quotations from the selections to support your points. 2. Are all kinds of courage the same? In what ways do different circumstances require different kinds of courage? Discuss these questions in a small group, referring to the selections for examples. 3. *The Diary of Anne Frank* gives readers a picture of courage from the inside—Anne wasn't writing about courage, she was just writing about her life. With this in mind, write several entries for the diary of another character, such as Rohan or a soldier in Henry V's army.

THEMATIC OPPORTUNITIES

Dreams and Ambition	
Big Question	**How do you bring a dream to life?** Everyone has a dream for their future, whether it is a job they'd love to have, a sport they want to play, a person they want to meet, or a place they'd love to travel. How do people go about making their dreams a reality? The selections in this grouping show how dreams and ambitions can guide someone to success.
Selections in the Anthology	• **"Raymond's Run,"** short story by Toni Cade Bambara, pp. 36–49 A young runner with promise chooses to refocus her energy on coaching her mentally impaired brother when she discovers that he has a talent and a passion for running, too. • **"The Spider Man Behind *Spider-Man*,"** feature article by Bijal P. Trivedi, pp. 890–899 Not many people have a passion for bugs. But Steven Kutcher does, and he has turned it into a fascinating career. • **"Interview with a Songcatcher,"** interview by Brian Handwerk, pp. 914–923 Henrietta Yurchenco has found that music can bridge any language barrier between people of different cultures. • **"One Last Time,"** memoir by Gary Soto, pp. 838–851 The author learns that hard work can really pay off.
Related Novels and Longer Works	***M. L. K.: Journey of a King,*** biography by Tonya Bolden The author describes the life of Dr. Martin Luther King Jr. and the role his belief in agape, the selfless love for one's neighbor, had in his life. ***I, Juan de Pareja,*** historical fiction by Elizabeth Borton de Treviño In this award-winning novel set in Spain during the 1600s, a Moorish man born into slavery seeks freedom and recognition as an artist. ***Heat,*** novel by Mike Lupica Cuban-born Michael Arroyo's home-life and his dreams are put in jeopardy when he is required to show his birth certificate in order to pitch in the Little League World Series.
Wrap-Up	To assess understanding, have students respond to one of these culminating options. 1. What kinds of sacrifices are worth making for your dreams? Discuss this question in small groups. Use details from these selections and others to support your opinions. 2. For each selection you read, create a word collage that illustrates the subject or main character's dreams. 3. The characters and people you read about all had ambition. Write an essay that examines the role ambition played in each person's life. What conclusions can you draw about the importance of ambition in achieving your dreams?

Lesson at a Glance

The Power of Ideas

WHY THIS UNIT?

In this Introductory Unit, students get a brief overview of the kinds of themes, literary genres, reading strategies, and writing skills they will study throughout the year. The unit gives them a preview of how their textbook is structured and how it approaches the study of literature and writing.

ABOUT THE WORKSHOPS

Student/Teacher's Edition Pages: 1–19

Summary   The unit begins by introducing students to some of the "big questions" they will consider as they read each selection in the anthology. Then, in the Genres Workshop, students learn the defining characteristics of fiction, poetry, drama, nonfiction, and media, as well as some of the academic vocabulary they will use to explore these genres. The Reading Strategies Workshop outlines eight basic skills and strategies that will help students become active readers. The Writing Process Workshop reviews the basics of writing, from identifying audience, purpose, and format to following the steps of the writing process and using a rubric for self-assessment.

Big Questions: The Power of Ideas The unit captures students' attention by pointing out that literature explores the big **questions** that affect every person's life. It explains that questions can be explored in a variety of genres, and that students can tap into these questions through active, engaged reading. Finally, the unit invites students to use the power of literature to express their own ideas through writing.

LESSON RESOURCES
Student Copy Masters

All lesson resources are available electronically on DVD-ROM

GENRES WORKSHOP   COPY MASTER
Note Taking

THE GENRES
Key Terms
Fill in the blanks and the chart to help you to remember the key terms.

GENRES

1. Fiction   Elements of fiction include _____ , _____ , _____ , and _____ .

    Theme is _____

    Forms of fiction:

    • **Short stories**, which are _____

    • **Novels**, which are _____

    • **Novellas**, which are _____

2. Poetry is _____ .

    Poetry is made up of _____ and _____ .

    The sound of a poem is created by devices such as _____ and _____ .

3. Drama is _____ .

    A **play** is divided into _____ and _____ .

    The plot and characters are developed through _____

    Stage directions describe _____

4. Nonfiction is _____

    Autobiographies and biographies both tell _____

    • A biography uses _____ point of view.

    • An autobiography uses _____ point of view.

    Essays are _____

    Speeches are _____

    News articles are _____

    Feature articles are _____

    Other informational nonfiction includes _____

5. Media refers to _____

    Types of Media include

    _____

    _____

    _____

    _____

    Being media literate means _____

READING STRATEGIES WORKSHOP

Note Taking

BECOMING AN ACTIVE READER

Directions: Complete the outline to help you remember the key terms from this workshop.

I. Before Reading

A. Active readers should preview a text

B. _____

II. During Reading

A. Use prior knowledge, or _____

B. Predict, or _____

C. Visualize, or _____

D. Monitor, or _____

E. Use details in the text to _____

III. After Reading

A. Ask questions to connect to a text

1. _____ ?

2. _____ ?

ACADEMIC VOCABULARY WORKSHOP

Note Taking

WHAT IS ACADEMIC VOCABULARY?

Directions: Take notes about Academic Vocbaulary by using the information on pages 16–19 to complete chart.

ACADEMIC VOCABULARY	
Definition of academic vocabulary	
Benefits of learning academic vocabulary	
Three examples of academic vocabulary	1. _____ 2. _____ 3. _____
Three strategies for building academic vocabulary	1. _____ 2. _____ 3. _____

WRITING PROCESS WORKSHOP

Note Taking

EXPRESSING IDEAS IN WRITING

Key Terms

Fill in the blanks to make complete sentences that will help you to remember the terms.

1. Before beginning to write, writers decide on the _____,

_____, and _____.

The Writing Process

The major steps in the writing process are

1. _____

2. _____

3. _____

4. _____

Fill in the chart to help you remember the key traits of effective writing.

Six key traits of effective writing	Examples of strong writing
•	•
•	•
•	•
•	•
•	•
•	•

Take notes as you read about writing strategies that work. Fill in the blanks to complete the sentences.

Writing Strategies

1. Writers use these three strategies to help them write: _____,

_____, and _____.

2. These prewriting strategies can help writers brainstorm ideas: _____,

_____, _____, or _____.

3. A writer should ask the peer reader _____.

4. A peer reader should _____.

The Main Events: Plot and Conflict

UNIT 1

Academic Vocabulary

A. Academic Vocabulary is the language you use to talk about literature. Listen as your teacher reads each word and discusses its meaning and the example sentence.

Academic Vocabulary	Definition	Example Sentence
1. affect	to have an effect on, to bring about a change	Practice can **affect** your performance.
2. conclude	to reach a decision	My reaction leads me to **conclude** that I am allergic to bananas.
3. evident	easily seen or understood	It is **evident** by the look on your face that you are enjoying the movie.
4. imply	to express indirectly	Your silence could **imply** interest or boredom.
5. initial	first; happening at the beginning	Your **initial** response was interest, but it then you became bored.

B. Use an Academic Vocabulary word to complete each sentence.

1. It is _____ by your wet clothes that it is raining outside.

2. The _____ chapter introduces the characters and sets up the story.

3. Too much food can _____ goldfish in a negative way.

4. Your wet clothes lead me to _____ that it is raining outside.

5. Their happy expressions _____ that they had a good time.

C. Write the Academic Vocabulary words in your Reader/Writer Notebook. Practice using these words as you talk and write about the selections in this unit.

UNIT 1   COPY MASTER

Additional Academic Vocabulary

A. Listen as your teacher reads each word and discusses its meaning and the example sentence.

Academic Vocabulary	Definition	Example Sentence
1. establish	to settle; fix; to begin or found a government, nation, company, etc.	We plan to **establish** a green club at our school.
2. estimate	to make a guess about the size, quality, value, or cost of; a guess	We **estimate** that 200 people will attend the show.
3. institute	to set up; establish; to start; enter upon; a school or organization for some special study	There is a new design **institute** in our town.
4. monitor	to listen to or watch in order to check up on	Scientists placed a tiny device on the geese to **monitor** their migration.
5. section	a part cut off; division; a distinct or separate part	There is a special seating **section** for parents.

B. Write a word from the chart to replace each underlined word or phrase in the following dialogue.

1. The city will <u>found</u> a new swimming pool next summer.

2. Officials <u>guess</u> that it will cost about a million dollars to build.

3. The plan to <u>set up</u> strict rules for using the pool.

4. They will create a <u>separate area</u> for babies and toddlers.

5. And they will hire a life guard to <u>watch</u> the swimmers.

Grammar Focus

These charts provide two methods of incorporating grammar instruction in your literature class. You may choose one approach, or blend the two.

Systematic Grammar Instruction: Nouns

Introducing the Unit: Students can start the academic year by reviewing one of the two most basic parts of speech.

Review	Grammar Handbook (See Student Edition)	Language Handbook
• *The Sentence and Its Parts*	Quick Reference: The Sentence and Its Parts, p. R48; The Sentence and Its Parts, p. R60	Identifying Subjects, Verbs, and Complements, p. 92
• *Kinds of Nouns*	Quick Reference: Noun, p. R46	Identifying Nouns, p. 1

Week	Grammar Handbook (See Student Edition)	Language Handbook
1 Singular and Plural Nouns	Singular and Plural Nouns, p. R52	—
2 Possessive Nouns	Possessive Nouns, p. R52	—
3 Compound Nouns	—	Identifying and Using Compound Subjects and Compound Verbs, p. 88
4 Nouns as Subjects and Complements	—	Identifying Subjects, Verbs, and Complements, p. 92
5 Nouns in Phrases	—	Identifying Prepositional Phrases, p. 65

Related Mechanics Topics	Grammar Handbook (See Student Edition)	Language Handbook
• Capitalization	Quick Reference: Capitalization, p. R51	Using Capital Letters Correctly, p. 127

Integrating Grammar, Literature, and Writing

Use activities provided in the literature selections and Writing Workshop to reinforce grammar concepts in the context of writing, revision, and author's style. You may extend or reinforce those lessons using Handbook lessons in the student edition or the *Language Handbook*.

Teaching Opportunities	Grammar Handbook (See Student Edition)	Language Handbook
Raymond's Run Avoid Sentence Fragments	Correcting Fragments, p. R64	Correcting Sentence Fragments, p. 84
The Ransom of Red Chief Avoid Run-On Sentences	Correcting Run-On Sentences, pp. R64–R65	Correcting Run-on Sentences, p. 107; Correcting and Revising Run-on Sentences, pp. 108–109
Clean Sweep Use Progressive Form Correctly	Progressive Forms, p. R56	Identifying and Using Verb Tenses, pp. 32–33
The Hitchhiker Maintain Pronoun-Antecedent Agreement	Pronouns: Agreement with Antecedent, pp. R52–R53	Ensuring Agreement Between Pronoun and Antecedent, p. 20
The Great Rat Hunt Use Past Perfect Tense Correctly	Verb Tense, p. R56	Identifying and Using Verb Tenses, pp. 32–33
Writing Workshop Personal Narrative Punctuating Verbs in a Series, Correcting Run-on Sentences	—	Using Commas to Separate Words and Phrases and After Introductory Elements, p. 139; Correcting Run-on Sentences, p. 107; Correcting and Revising Run-on Sentences, pp. 108–109

Essential Course of Study ECOS **Lesson at a Glance**

Text Analysis Workshop | Plot and Conflict

OVERVIEW AND PURPOSE

The following key terms and concepts are introduced in the Text Analysis Workshop for Unit 1. They will be reviewed and reinforced throughout the unit, and assessed on the Unit 1 Test.

- External Conflict
- Internal Conflict
- Stages of plot (exposition, rising action, climax, falling action, resolution)

WORKSHOP EXCERPTS

Johnny Tremain
novel by Esther Forbes

"Eva and the Mayor"
short story by Jean Davies Okimoto

"The Elevator"
short story by William Sleator

LESSON RESOURCES

Student Copy Masters

These copy masters may be used to provide note-taking support for students at lower readiness levels.

- Note Taking, p.7
- Note Taking, p.8

ℹ Lesson resources are also available on the **Teacher One Stop DVD-ROM** and online at <u>thinkcentral.com</u>.

TEXT ANALYSIS WORKSHOP: PART 1   COPY MASTER

Note Taking

CONFLICT—THE FUEL OF A STORY

Fill in the blanks to help you remember key information about conflict in a story.

1. In a story, a **conflict** is _____.

2. Two types of **conflict** are _____ and _____.

Fill in the two types of conflict to create the heads for this chart. Then add details about each type of conflict.

_____ Conflict	_____ Conflict
This kind of conflict involves a struggle between a _____ and an _____.	This kind of conflict takes place within _____.
Character vs. _____ Examples:	Character vs. _____ Examples:
Character vs. _____ Examples:	
Character vs. _____ Examples:	

TEXT ANALYSIS WORKSHOP: PART 2

Note Taking

STAGES OF PLOT

Fill in the blanks to make complete sentences that will help you remember the terms.

1. A **plot** is the _____ in a story.

2. In a traditional plot structure, there are _____ stages.

The stages of plot usually happen in this order:

1. In the **exposition,** the author introduces the _____ and the _____ and also reveals the story's _____.

2. The **rising action** is the part of the story that introduces _____ and builds _____.

3. The **climax** is _____. In this part of the story, the conflict is _____.

4. The **falling action** is the part of the story when the author reveals _____. It also _____ and _____.

5. The **resolution** is the part of the story that reveals _____ and _____.

RRRAAARAYMOND'S RRRUN

TONI CADE BAMBARA

WHY THIS SELECTION?

This short story by award-winning author Toni Cade Bambara presents sympathetic and relevant characters who deal with conflicts to which students can relate. The engaging plot provides opportunities to examine the concepts of ambition and motivation.

ABOUT THIS SELECTION

Student/Teacher's Edition Pages: 36–49
Difficulty Level Average
Readability Scores: Lexile: 1270; Fry: 7; Dale-Chall: 6.6

Summary Squeaky takes running very seriously. She takes her responsibility for her mentally impaired brother Raymond even more seriously. Raymond accompanies her everywhere, even on her training runs. During the big May Day race, as Squeaky dashes toward the finish line, she notices Raymond on the other side of the fence, running as hard as he can. Although Squeaky wins the race, she decides that she'll retire and devote herself to training Raymond.

Engaging the Students The narrator of this story experiences a shift in her motivation. As students read the story, they are challenged to think about what fuels their ambitions.

COMMON CORE STANDARDS FOCUS

- Plot
- Make Inferences

LESSON RESOURCES

Plan and Teach

Student Copy Masters

ℹ Lesson resources are also available on the **Teacher One Stop DVD-ROM** and online at thinkcentral.com.

Lesson Plan and Resource Guide

Raymond's Run
Short Story by Toni Cade Bambara

Common Core Focus

RL 1 Cite the evidence that supports inferences drawn from the text. **RL 3** Analyze how incidents in a story propel the action or provoke a decision. **W 2** Write informative texts. **L 1** Demonstrate command of standard English grammar when writing. **L 3** Use knowledge of language when writing. **L 6** Use accurately grade-appropriate words.

Unless otherwise noted, all resources can be found in the *Resource Manager*.
❶ Lesson resources are also available on the **Teacher One Stop DVD-ROM** and online at **thinkcentral.com**. The Student Edition and selected copy masters are available electronically on the ❷ **Student One Stop DVD-ROM**.

Student/Teacher's Edition Pages	Additional Resources CM = Copy Master T = Transparency
Focus and Motivate	
❑ Big Question p. 36	❑ ❶ **PowerNotes DVD-ROM** and online at **thinkcentral.com**
❑ Author Biography p. 37	❑ ❶ Literature and Reading Center at **thinkcentral.com**
Teach	
❑ Plot p. 37	❑ ❶ **PowerNotes DVD-ROM** and online at **thinkcentral.com**
❑ Make Inferences p. 37	❑ Make Inferences CM— English p. 21, Spanish p. 22 **D** ❑ ❶ **PowerNotes DVD-ROM** and online at **thinkcentral.com**
❑ Vocabulary in Context p. 37	❑ Vocabulary Study CM p. 23 **D** ❑ ❶ **PowerNotes DVD-ROM** and online at **thinkcentral.com**

D = Resources for Differentiation

Student/Teacher's Edition Pages	Additional Resources CM = Copy Master T = Transparency

Practice and Apply: Guided Practice

Selection and Teacher Notes

❏ "Raymond's Run," pp. 38–46

❏ 🎧 **Audio Anthology CD** Ⓓ
❏ Summary CM—English and Spanish p. 17, Haitian Creole and Vietnamese p. 18 Ⓓ
❏ Reading Fluency CM p. 29
❏ 💼 **Best Practices Toolkit**
❏ Read Aloud/Think Aloud p. A34 [T]
❏ Story Map p. D16 [T] Ⓓ
❏ Character Map p. D8 [T] Ⓓ
❏ ⓘ ThinkAloud Models at **thinkcentral.com**
❏ ⓘ Audio Summaries at **thinkcentral.com**

Practice and Apply: After Reading

❏ Selection Questions p. 47

❏ Reading Check CM p. 26
❏ Plot CM— English p. 19, Spanish p. 20 Ⓓ
❏ Question Support CM p. 27 Ⓓ
❏ Additional Selection Questions p. 13 Ⓓ
❏ Ideas for Extension p. 14 Ⓓ

❏ Vocabulary Practice p. 48
❏ Academic Vocabulary in Writing p. 48
❏ Vocabulary Strategy: Foreign Words in English p. 48

❏ Vocabulary Practice CM p. 24
❏ Academic Vocabulary CM p. 2
❏ Additional Academic Vocabulary CM p. 3
❏ Vocabulary Strategy CM p. 25
❏ ⓘ WordSharp Interactive Vocabulary Tutor CD-ROM and online at **thinkcentral.com**

❏ Grammar in Context p. 49
❏ Writing Prompt p. 49

❏ 💼 **Best Practices Toolkit**
❏ Reporter's Questions p. C9 [T] Ⓓ
❏ Avoid Sentence Fragments CM p. 28
❏ Grammar Handbook—Student Edition p. R64

Ⓓ = Resources for Differentiation

RAYMOND'S RUN

Student/Teacher's Edition Pages	Additional Resources CM = Copy Master T = Transparency
Assess and Reteach	
Assess	❏ **Diagnostic and Selection Tests** ❏ Selection Tests A, B/C pp. 23–24, 25–26 **D** ❏ ❶ ThinkCentral Online Assessment ❏ ✐ ExamView Test Generator on the **Teacher One Stop DVD-ROM**

Reteach
 ❏ Plot
 ❏ Make Inferences
 ❏ Avoid Sentence Fragments
	❏ ❶ Level Up Online Tutorials on **thinkcentral.com**
	 ❏ ❶ Reteaching Worksheets on **thinkcentral.com**
	     ❏ Literature Lesson 5: Elements of Plot
	     ❏ Reading Lesson 8: Making Inferences
	     ❏ Grammar Lesson 1: Avoiding Sentence Fragments

D = Resources for Differentiation

If you are following the *Essential Course of Study*, this selection may also be found in

- **Interactive Reader**
- **Adapted Interactive Reader**
- ✐ **Adapted Interactive Reader: Audio Tutor**
- **English Language Learner Adapted interactive Reader**

Additional Selection Questions

Differentiation Use these questions to provide customized practice with comprehension and critical thinking skills.

Easy

1. **What's worth the *EFFORT*?**
   What motivates Squeaky to practice breathing exercises and high-prancing down the street? (*Her desire to win and excel at running is the motivation behind her daily practice.*)

2. **Identify Plot Elements** What do you learn about Squeaky and Raymond in the exposition? (*You learn that Squeaky runs and that she takes care of Raymond.*)

Average

3. **What's worth the *EFFORT*?**
   Does Squeaky run for herself or to win the approval of others? Explain. (*Squeaky appears to run for herself. Although she is pleased by her peers' praise at the end of the race, she seems to be driven more by her own need to run than this external factor. Nor does her parents' approval motivate her, since her mother would obviously prefer that she do something else.*)

4. **Analyze Plot** What are some of the conflicts in the story? (*The major conflict is whether Squeaky will win the May Day race over Gretchen. Other conflicts include Squeaky's conflict with her mother, who doesn't really understand her desire to run and avoid the activities enjoyed by other girls, Squeaky's conflicts with anyone who makes fun of Raymond, and her conflict with Mr. Pearson, who would like her to let someone else win.*)

5. **Make Inferences** Why does Squeaky gain respect for Gretchen? (*Before, during, and after the race, Gretchen acts like a serious runner. Also, Squeaky may see her as an individual for the first time without her gang of friends.*)

Challenging

6. **Evaluate Plot** Would the story's ending have changed dramatically if Squeaky had lost the race? Explain. (*No. She doesn't even know whether she has won or lost before she makes her new plans to be Raymond's coach. Although her victory makes her decision seem more selfless, she was planning to go ahead.*)

7. **Make Inferences** Will Squeaky follow through on her plan with Raymond? Support your inference with evidence from the text. (*Squeaky proves throughout the story that she is dependable. Even though her priority is training, she takes Raymond along with her, because that is her job. Her rigorous practice schedule, including early morning runs, shows that she is self-disciplined.*)

Ideas for Extension

Differentiation These activities provide students with a variety of options for demonstrating understanding of lesson concepts.

EXPLORATIONS AND ACTIVITIES

ORIGINAL ILLUSTRATIONS: VISUALIZE CHARACTER AND PLOT

Discuss with students how descriptive some of the passages in the story are. For example, lines 193–209 paint a vivid picture of Squeaky's thoughts and feelings as she begins to run.

Ask students to skim the story and choose the passage that they can visualize most clearly. Ask them to illustrate what they see, incorporating the details from the text.

Have students display their illustrations. Ask class members to match each picture with the associated passage from the text and discuss how closely the drawings fit their own mental images.

READERS THEATER: INTERPRET STORY ELEMENTS

Assign students to small groups and have them prepare a Readers Theater presentation of the story. Suggest that they develop dialogue based on the parts of the story in which Squeaky encounters other characters. Encourage them to adapt and abridge other segments as well in order to create a tightly woven dramatic reading.

As the students rehearse, suggest ways for them to incorporate gestures as well as voice and facial expression. Groups may wish to practice together in order to give feedback to each other.

Have groups present their Readers Theaters. Ask students to discuss how hearing the story helps them to understand character and plot more clearly.

T-SHIRT DESIGN: EXPLORE KEY CONCEPT

Suppose Squeaky has been asked to design a T-shirt for participants in the May Day races to wear. Have students make inferences about what messages she might want to send about running and competition.

Then ask pairs of students to create one or two designs, complete with graphics and text. Encourage them to use colors and symbols to convey a mood and their ideas.

Give each pair an opportunity to explain and display their T-shirts. Ask the class to vote on the one that they think most closely expresses Squeaky's perspective.

ACCEPTANCE SPEECH: INTERPRET CHARACTER

Discuss what Squeaky might have said if she were asked to give an acceptance speech after winning the race.

Have students jot down ideas on note cards and compose a speech from Squeaky's perspective. They should keep in mind Squeaky's character as presented throughout the story. After students have written their speeches, have them practice in small groups and give each other feedback on voice volume, pace, expression, and articulation.

Ask students to present their speeches to the class. Have listening students fill out a checklist evaluation on each one.

INQUIRY AND RESEARCH

TRAINING MANUAL

Discuss with students how many different ways there are for runners to train.

Assign students to small groups to research different training techniques and evaluate the merit of the ones they discover. Then ask them to put together their own training manual, complete with daily and weekly schedules, explanations of equipment, and diagrams showing how to perform various exercises.

Students can introduce their workout routines in a short presentation to the class.

Pre-AP Challenge: Have students put together a workout video to accompany their manual. Their videos should include demonstrations of some of the exercises as well as charts showing the advantages of the program they have designed. Have students present their videos to the class.

WRITING

EXPLORE POINT OF VIEW: MONOLOGUE

Discuss with students how the point of view of the story influences their perception of characters and events. Because Squeaky is the narrator, she draws the readers into her version of what happens, but other characters might have different views. Ask students to write a monologue from another character's point of view. They might choose Gretchen or Squeaky's mother. Have students focus on an event or part of the story and express feelings and thoughts from the particular character's perspective. Students may wish to brainstorm a list of ideas to include before they begin to write.

EXAMINE STYLE: STORY EXPOSITION

As a class, reread and discuss lines 1–21. In those first lines, readers learn a great deal about the narrator, setting, and other characters indirectly as well as directly.

Have students write one or two paragraphs of an original story, using a first-person point of view to introduce characters and a setting. Encourage them to experiment with voice to find the one that suits the narrator they have created. Suggest that they outline what they wish to include before they begin to write.

Teacher Notes

Review and Evaluate Outcome

What did I want students to know or be able to do?

How successful was the lesson?

Evaluate Process

What worked?

• Strategies

• Resources

• Differentiation

What did not work? Why not?

Reflect

The next time I teach "Raymond's Run," what will I do differently? Why?

Plan Ahead

What must I do next?

Summary

RAYMOND'S RUN

Toni Cade Bambara

Setting: New York City, present day

Squeaky is a no-nonsense girl who is very serious about two things—running and caring for her brother Raymond. Although Raymond is older than Squeaky, his mental disability makes him childlike. Squeaky takes Raymond with her when she practices running, and she defends him against the teasing of other kids. Squeaky is proud of how fast she runs, and she is sure that she can beat everyone in the May Day race—even Gretchen. At the race, Squeaky runs as hard as she can, but she notices that Gretchen is keeping up with her. Then she notices that Raymond, who is running on the other side of the fence, is keeping up with her too. The two girls finish at almost the same time. While the judges decide the outcome of the race, Squeaky realizes that she is so proud of Raymond's run that it doesn't really matter to her if she wins.

LA CARRERA DE RAYMOND

Toni Cade Bambara

Escenario: Ciudad de Nueva York, época actual

Squeaky es una niña muy seria y es muy cumplida en dos cosas: correr y cuidar a su hermano Raymond. Aunque Raymond es más grande que Squeaky, sus problemas de aprendizaje hacen que se comporte como un niño. Squeaky lleva a Raymond con ella cuando entrena para sus carreras, y ella lo defiende de las bromas que le hacen los demás niños. Squeaky está orgullosa de lo rápido que corre y está segura de que puede ganarles a todos en la carrera del primero de mayo, hasta a Gretchen. En la carrera, Squeaky corre lo más rápido que puede pero nota que Gretchen mantiene su ritmo. Después se da cuenta de que Raymond, quien está corriendo del otro lado de la valla, mantiene el mismo ritmo que ella también. Las dos niñas terminan casi al mismo tiempo. Mientras los jueces deciden el resultado de la carrera, Squeaky se da cuenta de que está tan orgullosa de la carrera de Raymond que realmente no le importa si ella gana.

Summary

KOURI RAYMOND AN
Toni Cade Bambara
Espas ak tan: Vil Nouyòk, tan jodi a

Skwiki se yon ti fi ki trè serye nan de (2) bagay—kouri ak pran swen frè li Remon. Menm si Remon pi gran pase Skwiki, andikap mantal msye a fè li tankou timoun. Skwiki pran Remon avèk li lè l ap fè pratik kouri, epi li defann li kont fawouch lòt timoun yo. Skwiki fyè pou fason li kouri vit, epi li sèten li ka genyen tout moun – menm Gretchenn – nan kous May Day la. Nan kous la, Skwiki kouri otan li kapab, men li remake Gretchenn ap kouri menm jan ak li. Epi, li remake Remon, k ap kouri sou lòt bò baryè a, menm jan ak li tou. De (2) ti medam yo fini prèske menm lè. Pandan jij la ap deside rezilta kous la, Skwiki reyalize li tèlman fyè pou jan Remon kouri sa fè li pa tèlman sousye l twòp èske l ap genyen.

Cuộc chạy của Raymond
Toni Cade Bambara
Bối cảnh: Thành phố New York, thời hiện tại

Squeaky không phải là cô bé ngu dại, cô rất coi trọng việc trông nom và chăm sóc anh trai mình là Raymond. Mặc dù Raymond lớn hơn Squeaky, bệnh thiểu năng trí tuệ làm cho cậu như một đứa trẻ. Squeaky đưa Raymond theo khi cô tập chạy và bảo vệ anh để bọn trẻ khác không trêu chọc. Squeaky tự hào vì cô chạy rất nhanh, và cô chắc chắn rằng cô có thể chiến thắng tất cả mọi người trong ngày thi chạy Tháng 5—ngay cả Gretchen. Tại cuộc thi, Squeaky chạy cố hết sức mình, nhưng cô nhận thấy rằng Gretchen đang đuổi kịp cô. Cô để ý thấy Raymond đang chạy ở phía bên kia hàng rào, và cũng đuổi kịp cô. Hai cô gái đến đích gần như cùng một lúc. Khi trọng tài quyết định kết quả cuộc chạy đua, Squeaky nhận thấy rằng cô quá đỗi tự hào về cuộc chạy đua của Raymond đến mức cô chẳng quan tâm cô có chiến thắng hay không.

Name _____   Date _____

COPY MASTER

Text Analysis

PLOT

The series of events that happen in a story make up its **plot.** Most plots include the following parts or stages:

- **exposition:** introduces the main characters, setting, and sometimes the conflict
- **rising action:** increases tension and builds the conflict
- **climax:** the point of greatest interest, or the turning point, of the story
- **falling action:** shows the result of the climax and brings the story to a close
- **resolution:** reveals the final outcome and ties up loose ends

Directions: List the important events in the story. Number each event. Then plot the events on the graph, by writing the number of each event on the part of the graph that indicates the plot stage in which the event occurs.

Important Events

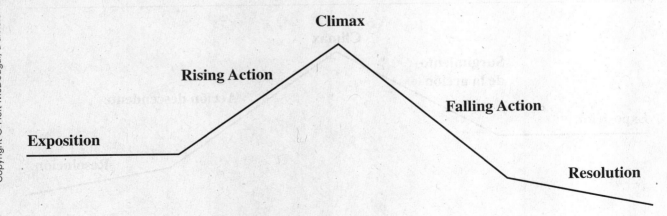

LA CARRERA DE RAYMOND

Text Analysis

PLOT

La serie de acontecimientos que suceden en un relato forman la **trama.** La mayoría de las tramas incluyen las siguientes partes o etapas.

- **Exposición:** presenta a los personajes principales, el escenario y algunas veces el conflicto.
- **Surgimiento de la acción:** aumenta la tensión y cimienta el conflicto.
- **Clímax:** el punto de mayor interés, o el punto decisivo de la historia.
- **Acción descendente:** muestra el resultado del clímax y lleva a la historia a una conclusión.
- **Resolución:** revela el resultado final y ata cabos sueltos.

Instrucciones: Haz una lista de los acontecimientos importantes del relato. Enumera cada acontecimiento. Después coloca los acontecimientos en la gráfica, escribiendo el número de cada acontecimiento en la parte de la gráfica que incluye la escena de la trama donde sucede el acontecimiento.

Acontecimientos importante

Climax

Surgimiento
de la acción

Acción descendente

Exposición

Resolución

RAYMOND'S RUN
Reading Skill

MAKE INFERENCES

When you **make inferences** while reading, you use clues from the story and your own knowledge to guess about things the author does not say directly.

Directions: As you read "Raymond's Run," record inferences you make about the main character's feelings, thoughts, and ideas in the graphic organizer. An example has been done for you.

Squeaky says her dad is the only one faster than she is.	+	Kids like when their parents are talented.	=	Squeaky is proud of her father.
	+		=	
	+		=	

RAYMOND'S RUN

LA CARRERA DE RAYMOND

Reading Skill

MAKE INFERENCES

Cuando **haces inferencias** mientras lees, usas claves del relato y tu propio conocimiento para especular sobre cosas que el autor no dice directamente.

Instrucciones: Mientras lees "La carrera de Raymond", anota las inferencias que haces sobre los sentimientos, pensamientos e ideas del personaje principal en el organizador gráfico. Sigue el ejemplo.

Squeaky dice que sólo su papa es más rápido que ella.	**+** A los niños les gusta que sus padres sean talentosos.	**=** Squeaky está orgullosa de su padre.
	+	**=**
	+	**=**

SPANISH

RAYMOND'S RUN

Vocabulary Study

SELF-ASSESSMENT OF WORD MEANING

A. Directions: As your teacher reads each set of sentences, listen for the boldfaced word and clues to its possible meaning.

1. She flexed her fingers so that she could **clutch** the baton firmly when she ran past her partner.

2. She perfected her **crouch**—low to the ground but balanced enough to allow her to push off strongly.

3. The race is **liable** to be very close. All of the runners perform well under pressure and have won before.

4. She may be a **prodigy,** but her talent cannot compensate for her consistent lack of effort.

5. Often in a **relay,** the fastest member of the team is the last runner. That way he or she can make up any time lost by the first runners.

6. Mary Louise followed Gretchen everywhere. No wonder everyone called her Gretchen's **sidekick.**

B. Directions: To determine how well you understand each vocabulary word, fill in the chart. As you read the selection, revise your definitions as needed.

Vocabulary Word	New	Seen Before	Can Use in a Sentence	Possible Meanings
1. clutch				
2. crouch				
3. liable				
4. prodigy				
5. relay				
6. sidekick				

RAYMOND'S RUN

RAYMOND'S RUN   COPY MASTER

Vocabulary Practice

clutch	crouch	liable	prodigy	relay	sidekick

A. Directions: Write the word from the box that best completes each sentence.

1. At the start of a race, the runners _____ down and place both hands on the ground in front of them.

2. The soloist was a _____ who had been performing with well-known orchestras since the age of ten.

3. The water was so rough that she had to _____ the sides of the small boat to keep from falling overboard.

4. If you don't step carefully, you are _____ to slip and fall.

5. Josie has a _____ who follows everywhere she goes.

6. Usually the best runner on the team is asked to run last in a _____ race.

B. Directions: Answer each question by writing one of the words from the box in the blank.

1. What is a synonym for *grasp?* _____

2. What is another word for *buddy* or *pal?* _____

3. How would you describe a person who has exceptional talent? _____

4. What type of race uses several members, each of whom finishes a part of the race?

   _____

5. What does a cat do before it leaps? _____

6. Which word means the same as *likely?* _____

RAYMOND'S RUN   COPY MASTER

Vocabulary Strategy

FOREIGN WORDS IN ENGLISH

The English language includes words from diverse languages, including French, German, Spanish, Japanese, and many others.

A. Directions: Use your knowledge of other cultures to choose which of the options provided state the origins of the boldfaced words. Write the name of the culture on the line. If you need help, you can look up the words in a dictionary.

1. I never leave for a vacation without my favorite **pajamas.** (Indian, French)

_____

2. The tourists were amazed at the disaster that the **tsunami** left behind. (Spanish, Japanese)

_____

3. The couple received an antique **casserole** from the bride's grandmother. (Italian, French)

_____

4. I dream of one day displaying my art in a famous art **gallery** for all to see. (Italian, African)

_____

5. This year we'll have a newly renovated **cafeteria** with a section for gelato. (German, Spanish)

_____

B. Directions: Choose **three** words from Exercise A. Write three sentences using one of the words in each sentence.

1. _____

_____

2. _____

_____

3. _____

_____

RAYMOND'S RUN

Reading Check

Directions: Recall all characters and events in the story. Then answer each question in sentences or phrases.

1. Why does Squeaky have to spend so much time watching out for her brother? How does she feel about that?

_____

_____

_____

2. How does Squeaky practice her running?

_____

_____

_____

3. Who is Gretchen?

_____

_____

_____

4. What does Squeaky's encounter with Gretchen, Rosie, and Mary Louise tell you about Squeaky?

_____

_____

_____

5. How does the race change what is important to Squeaky?

_____

_____

_____

Question Support

TEXT ANALYSIS

For questions 1–3, see page 47 of the Student Edition.

Directions: Answer each question.

4. Make Inferences Think about Squeaky's words and actions. Circle the details that best describe her.

    a. serious about running   **d.** protective of her brother

    b. has many close friends   **e.** expects to be treated with respect

    c. wins spelling bees   **f.** plays the piano well

5. Compare and Contrast Use the chart to show two ways that Squeaky and Gretchen are alike and two ways they are different.

Similarities	Differences

6. Analyze Plot Name an event that happens at each stage of the plot.

    Exposition _____

    Rising Action _____

    Climax _____

    Falling Action and Resolution _____

7. Draw Conclusions

    Tell how Squeaky views competition at the beginning of the story. _____

    _____

    How does Squeaky's attitude toward competition change after the May Day race? _____

    _____

8. Evaluate Plot Complete the following sentence.

    "Raymond's Run" has a realistic ending to me because _____

    _____

Grammar in Context

AVOID SENTENCE FRAGMENTS

A **sentence fragment** is an incomplete sentence. It is missing a subject, a predicate, or both. To fix, or complete, the sentence, the missing part or parts must be added.

Original: My brother Raymond. *(This is a sentence fragment because it is missing a predicate.)* He is older than I am.

Revised: My brother Raymond is older than I am. *(This is now a complete sentence.)*

Directions: Decide whether the following sentence fragments in bold are missing a subject, a predicate, or both. Combine each fragment with its accompanying complete sentence, inserting any missing words as necessary.

1. I left my books. **On the table.**

_____

_____

2. **The track meet.** It is the last event in the program.

_____

_____

3. I held my breath. **During the announcement.**

_____

_____

4. I love to run. **Can't get enough of it.**

_____

_____

5. The man with the loudspeaker called my name. **Then called Gretchen's.**

_____

_____

Reading Fluency

TRACKING SILENT READING RATE AND ACCURACY

Directions: The passage that follows provides information about the Special Olympics. Use this passage with the activity on page 30. Follow the directions on that page.

Eunice Kennedy Shriver founded the Special Olympics in 1968. The young people and adults who take part in the Special Olympics are intellectually disabled. Still, they learn how to swim, run long distances, race on snowshoes, play softball and soccer, lift weights, skate, and paddle kayaks. There are 30 individual and team events in which participants can compete.

Many cities and towns in the United States hold Special Olympics each year. The winners then go to state races and contests. The state winners in turn go on to the national games. Finally, the U.S. champions face champions from other countries. The first Special Olympics World Games were held in Chicago, Illinois. Since then, the games have been held in such countries as China, Ireland, Japan, and Morocco. In 2009, the World Games will return to the United States. They will be held in Boise, Idaho.

Many volunteers work for the Special Olympics. Some people work a few hours every week. Others volunteer for just one special event. People who are good at a sport might want to coach a team. If not, they can help with advertising or organizing. Those still in high school or in college are not too young to help out. In fact, the Special Olympics welcomes teenage volunteers.

The motto of the Special Olympics is: "Let me win, but, if I cannot win, let me be brave in the attempt." The Special Olympics are not just about winning. They are about trying your best. (248 words)

RAYMOND'S RUN

RAYMOND'S RUN

Reading Fluency

TRACKING SILENT READING RATE AND ACCURACY, CONTINUED

When you read silently, let your mind relax and take in the words. Move your eyes quickly across the page. Try to read groups of words as phrases. To increase your speed, use your hand as a marker to draw your eyes down the page.

Directions: Read the passage on page 29 silently. Have your partner time you and record your time on the chart. Your goal is to read at least 237 words correctly per minute. Then answer the questions 1–3. Repeat these steps two times. Try to increase your speed and understanding with each reading. Then evaluate your reading using questions 4 and 5.

Reading	1	2	3
Total Reading Time			

Check Your Understanding

1. Name three types of Special Olympic sports.

   _____

   _____

   _____

2. Who takes part in the Special Olympics?

   _____

   _____

3. Explain the motto of the Special Olympics.

   _____

   _____

   _____

Evaluate Your Fluency

1. How did repeated reading affect your speed?

   _____

   _____

2. Summarize the effect of repeated readings on your understanding of the passage.

   _____

   _____

RAYMOND'S RUN

THE RANSOM OF RED CHIEF

O. HENRY

WHY THIS SELECTION?

O. Henry stories challenge students while keeping them entertained. This selection is no exception, presenting a classic O. Henry twist at the end of a humorous narration.

ABOUT THIS SELECTION

Student/Teacher's Edition Pages: 50–65
Difficulty Level: Challenging
Readability Scores: Lexile: 980; Fry: 9; Dale-Chall: 7.9

Summary Con men Bill and Sam kidnap the son of a prominent citizen in a small town and hold him for a $2,000 ransom. The boy, who insists on being called Red Chief, terrorizes Bill until Bill begs Sam to reduce the ransom. In reply to the ransom note, the boy's father offers to take his son back if the men will pay him $250. The men agree and happily leave the boy, their money, and the town behind.

Engaging the Students This story offers students an opportunity to explore the key idea of the unexpected. As students read the story, they might consider the way life takes unexpected turns and whether one can ever prepare for all of them.

COMMON CORE STANDARDS FOCUS

• Conflict and Resolution
• Predict

LESSON RESOURCES

Plan and Teach

ℹ Lesson resources are also available on the **Teacher One Stop DVD-ROM** and online at <u>thinkcentral.com</u>.

THE RANSOM OF RED CHIEF

Lesson Plan and Resource Guide

The Ransom of Red Chief
Short Story by O. Henry

Common Core Focus

RL 3 Analyze how dialogue or incidents in a story propel the action and reveal aspects of a character.
W 2 Write explanatory texts. **L 1** Demonstrate command of standard English grammar when writing.
L 2 Demonstrate command of punctuation when writing. **L 4b** Use common Latin affixes as clues to the meaning of a word. **L 5b** Use the relationship between particular words to better understand each word.
L 6 Use accurately grade-appropriate words.

Unless otherwise noted, all resources can be found in the *Resource Manager*.
❶ Lesson resources are also available on the **Teacher One Stop DVD-ROM** and online at **thinkcentral.com.** The Student Edition and selected copy masters are available electronically on the ✐ **Student One Stop DVD-ROM.**

Student/Teacher's Edition Pages	Additional Resources CM = Copy Master T = Transparency
Focus and Motivate	
❑ Big Question p. 50	❑ ❶ **PowerNotes DVD-ROM** and online at **thinkcentral.com**
❑ Author Biography p. 51	❑ ❶ Literature and Reading Center at **thinkcentral.com**
Teach	
❑ Conflict and Resolution p. 51	❑ ❶ **PowerNotes DVD-ROM** and online at **thinkcentral.com**
❑ Predict p. 51	❑ Predict CM— English p. 43, Spanish p. 44 🅓 ❑ ❶ **PowerNotes DVD-ROM** and online at **thinkcentral.com**
❑ Vocabulary in Context p. 51	❑ Vocabulary Study CM p. 45 🅓 ❑ ❶ **PowerNotes DVD-ROM** and online at **thinkcentral.com**

🅓 = Resources for Differentiation

THE RANSOM OF RED CHIEF

Student/Teacher's Edition Pages	Additional Resources CM = Copy Master T = Transparency
Practice and Apply: Guided Practice	

Selection and Teacher Notes
❑ "The Ransom of Red Chief," pp. 52–61
❑ "Manuscript Found in an Attic," p. 62
	❑ 🔊 **Audio Anthology CD** Ⓓ
	❑ Summary CM—English and Spanish p. 39, Haitian Creole and Vietnamese p. 40 Ⓓ
	❑ Reading Fluency CM p. 51
	❑ 🧰 **Best Practices Toolkit**
	    ❑ T Chart p. A25 [T]
	    ❑ Making Inferences p. A13 [T] Ⓓ
	❑ ❶ ThinkAloud Models at **thinkcentral.com**
	❑ ❶ Audio Summaries at **thinkcentral.com**

Practice and Apply: After Reading	
❑ Selection Questions p. 63	❑ Reading Check CM p. 48 ❑ Conflict and Resolution CM— English p. 41, Spanish p. 42 Ⓓ ❑ Question Support CM p. 49 Ⓓ ❑ Additional Selection Questions p. 35 Ⓓ ❑ Ideas for Extension p. 36 Ⓓ
❑ Vocabulary Practice p. 64 ❑ Academic Vocabulary in Speaking p. 64 ❑ Vocabulary Strategy: The Prefix *com* and *multi-* p. 64	❑ Vocabulary Practice CM p. 46 ❑ Academic Vocabulary CM p. 2 ❑ Additional Academic Vocabulary CM p. 3 ❑ Vocabulary Strategy CM p. 47 ❑ ❶ *WordSharp* Interactive Vocabulary Tutor CD-ROM and online at **thinkcentral.com**
❑ Grammar in Context p. 65 ❑ Writing Prompt p. 65	❑ Avoid Run-On Sentences CM p. 50 ❑ Grammar Handbook—Student Edition p. R64 ❑ ❶ GrammarNotes DVD-ROM at **thinkcentral.com** ❑ ❶ Interactive Revision Lessons on WriteSmart CD-ROM and online at **thinkcentral.com**

Ⓓ = Resources for Differentiation

Student/Teacher's Edition Pages	Additional Resources CM = Copy Master T = Transparency
Assess and Reteach	
Assess	❑ **Diagnostic and Selection Tests** ❑ Selection Tests A, B/C pp. 27–28, 29–30 **D** ❑ **❶** ThinkCentral Online Assessment ❑ **✎** ExamView Test Generator on the **Teacher One Stop DVD-ROM**

Reteach
 ❑ Conflict and Resolution
 ❑ Predict
 ❑ Prefixes
 ❑ Avoid Run-On Sentences
	❑ **❶** Level Up Online Tutorials on **thinkcentral.com**
	 ❑ **❶** Reteaching Worksheets on **thinkcentral.com**
	     ❑ Literature Lesson 6: Conflict
	     ❑ Reading Lesson 1: Predicting
	     ❑ Reading Lesson 8: Making Inferences
	     ❑ Vocabulary Lesson 4: Prefixes
	     ❑ Grammar Lesson 2: Avoiding Run-Ons

D = Resources for Differentiation

If you are following the *Essential Course of Study*, this selection may also be found in

- **Interactive Reader**
- **Adapted Interactive Reader**
- **✎ Adapted Interactive Reader: Audio Tutor**
- **English Language Learner Adapted interactive Reader**

Additional Selection Questions

Use to supplement the questions on SE page 63.

Differentiation Use these questions to provide customized practice with comprehension and critical thinking skills.

Easy

1. **Is any plan *FOOLPROOF*?**
   What advance planning did Sam do to try to avoid unexpected problems? (*Sam and Bill found a cave and stocked it with provisions. They surveyed the town and decided on their victim. Sam rented a buggy from a different town so that it would not be traced to him.*)

2. **Identify Conflict and Resolution** Do Bill and Sam solve the conflict that inspired them to think of the kidnapping plan? (*No. They leave Summit without the money they need for their land scheme.*)

Average

3. **Is any plan *FOOLPROOF*?**
   What do the unexpected events that Sam and Bill encounter reveal about their characters? (*Sam copes well. He adjusts plans to meet changed circumstances, for example, lowering the ransom demand in order to get Red Chief back to his father. He stays relatively calm throughout. Bill, however, bears the brunt of the unexpectedly difficult and obnoxious kidnap victim, and as a result, he loses his nerve.*)

4. **Analyze Conflict and Resolution** Does the major conflict remain the same throughout the story? Explain. (*The conflict involves Bill, Sam, and Red Chief throughout. However, what they are in conflict over changes. The initial conflict is whether Bill and Sam can kidnap and keep Red Chief hostage long enough to successfully collect ransom money. Then it becomes a question of whether they can tolerate keeping him hostage for much longer with or without the ransom.*)

5. **Predict** Do you think that Bill and Sam will try kidnapping again? Why or why not? (*Students will most likely say that Bill and Sam's kidnapping days are behind them. They end up paying money instead of making money and have such a difficult time with their victim that they would be nervous to try again.*)

Challenging

6. **Evaluate Conflict and Resolution** Is the resolution of the major conflict satisfying? Why or why not? (*Yes. It maintains the humor and irony that runs throughout the story. It completes the picture of the two men as inept and harmless.*)

7. **Predict** Based on Red Chief's behavior in this story, what kind of adult do you think he will be? Support your answer with evidence from the text. (*Red Chief takes control of situations even as a ten-year old. So as an adult, he will probably be the one in charge and directing others to do what he wishes.*)

Ideas for Extension

Differentiation These activities provide students with a variety of options for demonstrating understanding of lesson concepts.

EXPLORATIONS AND ACTIVITIES

CHART EFFECTS: EXPLORE SETTING

Discuss with students how setting is more important in some stories than in others. Ask them to think about the ways that the time and place of this story affect the development of the plot.

Then have students work in small groups to create a cause-and-effect chart. The chart should identify aspects of the setting and examine their effects on the action. Encourage students to be specific in their analyses.

After the groups share their charts, talk about how the story would be different if it took place today.

DIAGRAM: TRACE PLOT

Students should skim the story, identifying significant events in the plot. Then ask them to collaborate on a plot diagram. Their diagram should include the exposition, rising action, climax, falling action, and resolution. Encourage them to draw their diagram on poster board. As a class, discuss and resolve any differences among students' diagrams.

Pre-AP Challenge: Ask students to imagine an additional event for the story, and work it into their plot diagram, either in the rising or falling action. They should identify where their event belongs on the diagram and include a description. Encourage students to make their events ironic or funny, in keeping with the rest of the story. Have students share their diagrams and plot additions.

DIALOGUE: ANALYZE CHARACTER

As a class, speculate about the conversation that Bill and Sam might have had after they left Summit. What would they have been feeling? What would they have said about the experience and about their future plans?

Students should then create a possible dialogue between the two characters. Ask them to first identify the ideas that they want to include in the conversation and then to skim the story to get a sense of the speech patterns of both Sam and Bill. Encourage them to make the dialogue as close to the original as possible.

Have students perform their dialogues for the class. Ask listening students to evaluate the strengths of each performance.

COMIC STRIP: INTERPRET PLOT

Point out that many of the events in this story could become the basis for a comic strip. The humor, irony, and characterization lend themselves well to that medium.

Ask students to work in pairs and develop a comic strip based on one of the episodes in the story. Suggest that they choose an incident that has a beginning and an end and that provides them with ideas for illustrations as well as dialogue.

Have students present their comic strips on large sheets of paper or posters. Display them around the room in the order in which the events occur in the story.

READ STORIES: COMPARE AND CONTRAST ELEMENTS OF FICTION

Tell students that many of O. Henry's stories have surprising endings. Ask students to read another short story by O. Henry, such as "The Gift of the Magi" or "Hearts and Hands."

As they read, have them compare and contrast the plot, the characters, and the style of "The Ransom of Red Chief" with those of the second story. Ask students to share their comparisons and discuss which story they liked better and why.

INQUIRY AND RESEARCH

LIFE OF O. HENRY

Have students reread the introduction to O. Henry's life on page 51 of their textbooks. Point out that there is much information about the author that is left untold, including some of the stories behind the events in his life.

Students should use the Internet and print resources to find out more about O. Henry and unravel some of the mysteries in his life. Then ask them to write a short biographical article using the information they find. Have them read their articles to the class and compare notes.

WRITING

EXPLORE POINT OF VIEW: JOURNAL ENTRY

How would Mr. Dorset view the kidnapping episode? Have students consider his actions as well as what he writes in the note in order to make inferences about his reaction. Then ask them to write a journal entry from his perspective about his experiences. Remind students to maintain first-person point of view.

SUMMARIZE: NEWSPAPER REPORT

A newspaper report about a kidnapping would probably sound very different from a humorous story like this one. Ask students to think of how this incident might be reported in a newspaper. The report should include information about the disappearance of Red Chief, efforts made to find him, contact with the kidnappers, and his mysterious reappearance. As students write up the article, suggest that they consider what a reporter would and would not know about all of the aspects of the event.

THE RANSOM OF RED CHIEF

Teacher Notes

Review and Evaluate Outcome

What did I want students to know or be able to do?

How successful was the lesson?

Evaluate Process

What worked?

• Strategies

• Resources

• Differentiation

What did not work? Why not?

Reflect

The next time I teach "The Ransom of Red Chief," what will I do differently? Why?

Plan Ahead

What must I do next?

THE RANSOM OF RED CHIEF

Summary

THE RANSOM OF RED CHIEF

O. Henry

Setting: Alabama, early 1900s

Sam and Bill are two crooks who need two thousand dollars in order to cheat some townspeople in Illinois out of their land. To raise the money, they kidnap Johnny Dorset, the son of a rich man in a small town in Alabama. They take the boy to a cave outside of town. The story is narrated by Sam, who tells how the red-headed, ten-year-old boy terrorizes the two kidnappers. Johnny, who wants to be called Red Chief, thinks this is all a fine adventure. The boy decides that Bill is his captive and calls him Old Hank the Trapper. He calls Sam Snake-eye the Spy. After one night with the boy, both men are covered with bruises. Even worse, Red Chief nearly scalps Bill and threatens to burn Sam at the stake. By the time Sam and Bill write the ransom note, they are so eager to get rid of Red Chief that they reduce their demand to fifteen hundred dollars. While Sam goes to deliver the ransom note, Red Chief continues to make trouble for Bill. In desperation, Bill tries to send the boy home, but Red Chief refuses to go—he's having too much fun. Finally, Sam picks up the answer to the ransom note, but it is not at all what they had expected.

EL RESCATE DEL JEFE ROJO

O. Henry

Escenario: Alabama, principios del s. XX

Sam y Bill son dos bandidos que necesitan dos mil dólares para estafar a unos habitantes de Illinois y quitarles su tierra. Para conseguir el dinero, secuestran a Johnny Dorset, el hijo de un hombre rico de un pueblo pequeño en Alabama. Ellos se llevan al niño a una cueva afuera del pueblo. Sam narra la historia, y cuenta cómo el pelirrojo de diez años aterroriza a los dos secuestradores. Johnny, quien quiere hacerse llamar Jefe Rojo, piensa que esta es una gran aventura. El niño decide que Bill es su cautivo y lo llama Viejo Hank el Trampero. A Sam lo nombra el Espía Ojo de Víbora. Después de una noche con el niño, los dos hombres están cubiertos de moretones. Peor aún, el Jefe Rojo casi le quita el cuero cabelludo a Bill y amenaza con quemar a Sam en la hoguera. Para cuando Sam y Bill escriben la nota de rescate, están tan ansiosos por deshacerse del Jefe Rojo que reducen el monto del rescate a mil quinientos dólares. Mientras Sam va a entregar la nota de rescate, el Jefe Rojo continúa causándole problemas a Bill. Desesperado, Bill trata de enviar al niño a casa, pero el Jefe Rojo se rehúsa a irse; se está divirtiendo mucho. Finalmente, Sam recoge la respuesta a la nota de rescate, pero no es para nada lo que ellos esperaban.

Summary

RANSON RED CHIEF

O. Henry
Espas ak tan: Alabama, kòmansman ane 1900 yo

Sam ak Bil se de (2) kriminèl ki bezwen de (2) mil dola pou yo kapab chèche pran tè kèk moun lavil nan Ilinòy. Pou yo jwenn lajan an, yo kidnape Djonni Dòsèt, pitit gason yon nonm rich ki nan yon ti vil nan Alabama. Yo mete ti gason an nan yon gwòt ki deyò vil la. Sam ki rakonte istwa a di kouman ti gason dizan an sa a ki gen cheve wouj fè de (2) kidnapè yo gen laperèz. Djonni, ki vle pou yo rele l Red Chief, panse sa a se yon bèl avanti. Ti gason an deside pou Bil se prizonye li epi li rele li Old Hand, Trapè a. Li rele Sam Espyon zye Sèpan an. Apre yon nwit avèk ti gason an, toulède mesye yo plen mak sou po yo. Sa ki pi rèd la, Red Chief manke dekale po Bil epi li menase pou li boule Sam nan yon poto. Nan moman Sam ak Bil ap ekri nòt ranson an, yo tèlman gen dezi pou yo debarase yo avèk Red Chief, yo diminye demann yo ak kenz mil dola. Pandan Sam pral pote nòt ranson an ale, Red Chief kontinye kreye pwoblèm pou Bil. Bil vin pèdi lespwa, kidonk li voye ti gason an lakay li, men Red Chief refize ale—li pran twòp plezi. Finalman, Sam al pran repons pou nòt ranson an, men se pa t a yon bagay kon sa yo te atann yo ditou.

Tiền chuộc Sếp Đỏ

O. Henry
Bối cảnh: Alabama, đầu những năm 1900

Sam và Bill là hai kẻ lừa gạt, chúng cần 2000 đô la để lừa một số người dân thị trấn ở Illinois để lấy đất của họ. Để có tiền, chúng bắt cóc Johnny Dorset, con trai của một người đàn ông giàu có ở một thị trấn nhỏ ở Alabama. Chúng đưa cậu bé vào một cái hang ở ngoài thị trấn. Câu chuyện do Sam kể lại, hắn kể cậu bé mười tuổi đầu đỏ khủng bố hai tên bắt cóc như thế nào. Johnny, muốn được gọi là Sếp Đỏ, nghĩ đây là một cuộc phiêu lưu hay. Cậu bé quyết định rằng Bill là tù nhân của cậu và gọi hắn là Vòng sắt cũ, kẻ Đánh bẫy. Gọi Sam là Mắt rắn, tên Gián điệp. Sau một đêm với cậu bé, hai người đàn ông mình đầy vết thâm tím. Tệ hơn nữa, Sếp Đỏ gần như lột da đầu Bill và dọa thiêu Sam trong khi đang bị lâm nguy. Khi Sam và Bill viết giấy hẹn trả tiền chuộc, chúng rất muốn tống khứ Sếp Đỏ đi để chúng giảm yêu cầu của chúng xuống 1500 đô la. Khi Sam đi đưa giấy hẹn trả tiền chuộc, Sếp Đỏ tiếp tục gây rắc rối cho Bill. Vào thế cùng, Bill cố đưa cậu bé về nhà, nhưng Sếp đỏ không chịu đi—cậu đang quá vui vẻ. Cuối cùng, Sam đi lấy câu trả lời cho giấy hẹn trả tiền chuộc, nhưng đó không phải là tất cả những gì chúng mong đợi.

THE RANSOM OF RED CHIEF

Text Analysis

CONFLICT AND RESOLUTION

A story's plot centers on **conflicts,** or struggles between opposing forces. By the end of the story, the conflicts are usually **resolved,** or settled. When an outcome is the opposite of what might be expected, it is said to be **ironic.**

Directions: Use the graphic to record conflicts in "The Ransom of Red Chief." Note expected and actual resolutions, and indicate whether or not each outcome is ironic.

Conflict:

Expected Resolution:

Actual Resolution:

Ironic?

Conflict:

Expected Resolution:

Actual Resolution:

Ironic?

THE RANSOM OF RED CHIEF

EL RESCATE DEL JEFE ROJO

Text Analysis

CONFLICT AND RESOLUTION

La trama de un relato se centra en los **conflictos,** o luchas entre fuerzas opuestas. Al final del relato, los conflictos generalmente están **resueltos,** o terminados. Cuando el resultado es lo opuesto a lo que se esperaba se dice que ese resultado es **irónico.**

Instrucciones: Usa la gráfica para registrar los conflictos en "El rescate del Jefe Rojo". Anota resoluciones reales y esperadas e indica si el resultado es irónico.

Conflicto:

Resolución esperada: **Resolución real:**

¿Irónico?

Conflicto:

Resolución esperada: **Resolución real:**

¿Irónico?

SPANISH

Resource Manager

THE RANSOM OF RED CHIEF

Reading Strategy

PREDICT

If you try to guess what will happen next when you read a story or watch a TV show, you are making **predictions.** To predict events or outcomes, use clues from the text and your own common sense. You may need to change your predictions as you uncover new information.

Directions: As you read "The Ransom of Red Chief," write your predictions in the chart. Then record the actual event and tell whether your prediction was correct or whether the actual event surprised you. An example has been done for you.

My Prediction	Actual Event	Correct or Surprised?
The boy will fight back when kidnapped.	Boy fights back	correct

THE RANSOM OF RED CHIEF

EL RESCATE DEL JEFE ROJO

Reading Strategy

PREDICT

Si tratas de adivinar lo que sucederá a continuación cuando lees un relato o miras un programa de televisión, estás haciendo **predicciones.** Para predecir acontecimientos o desenlaces, usa las claves del texto y de tu propio sentido común. Es posible que necesites cambiar tus predicciones a medida que descubras nueva información.

Instrucciones: A medida que leas "El rescate del Jefe Rojo", escribe tus predicciones en la gráfica. Después anota el acontecimiento real y menciona si tu predicción fue correcta o si el acontecimiento real te sorprendió. Sigue el ejemplo.

Mi predicción	Acontecimiento real	¿Fue correcta o tuviste una sorpresa?
El niño peleaba cuando lo secuestraron.	el niño pelea.	correcta

SPANISH

THE RANSOM OF RED CHIEF

Vocabulary Study

WORD QUESTIONING

A. Directions: As your teacher reads each sentence, listen for the boldfaced word. On a separate sheet of paper, work together to create a word map like the one shown. Fill in as much information as you can.

1. One person alone could not complete the project in time, so they needed to **collaborate.**

2. He felt his scheme should **commend** itself to professional kidnappers because it was so well planned.

3. If Mr. Dorset did not **comply** with the demands, he would not see Red Chief again.

4. The **diatribe** denouncing the villains appeared in the paper the next day.

5. The boy was **impudent,** answering back rudely whenever he was asked a question.

6. The father considered the **proposition** and then sent back his own suggestion.

7. The kidnappers stocked the cave with enough **provisions** to last them a week.

8. The note requested that the **ransom** be paid promptly and in large bills.

Part of word I recognize		I think it means . . .
It is . . .	Word in Context	It is not . . .
Related words		Examples of

B. Directions: Based on your discussion of the boldfaced words and the Key Idea for "The Ransom of Red Chief" explain how the boldfaced words might fit into an essay about the unexpected.

_____

_____

_____

_____

THE RANSOM OF RED CHIEF

COPY MASTER

Vocabulary Practice

collaborate	comply	impudent	provisions
commend	diatribe	proposition	ransom

A. Directions: Write the word from the box that best completes each sentence.

1. Because the job is difficult, we have asked several departments to

_____ to find a solution.

2. After the art show, people sought out the painter to _____ her
for her work.

3. He was prepared for good-natured criticism of his work, but he did not expect

the _____ that appeared in the newspaper.

4. The students came up with their own _____ for raising money
for the class trip.

5. The public was advised to prepare for the hurricane by stocking up on

_____ like water and canned goods.

6. We were shocked at the _____ behavior of the child, who showed
no respect for his parents or his teacher.

7. The kidnappers demanded a _____ for the return of the child.

8. If you do not _____ with the rules, you will not be allowed to
participate in the game.

B. Directions: Fill in each blank with an antonym from the word box.

1. praise _____

2. polite _____

3. disapprove _____

4. resist _____

THE RANSOM OF RED CHIEF   COPY MASTER

Vocabulary Strategy

THE PREFIX com- AND multi-

The vocabulary word *commend* contains the prefix *com-*, which means "together" or "with." The prefix can be spelled *com-*, *col-*, *con-*, or *cor-*, depending on the letter that follows it. Learning to recognize this prefix with its various spellings can help you determine the meaning of many words. Another common prefix is *multi-*, which means "more than one."

A. Directions: Choose a word from the box to complete each sentence. Refer to a dictionary if you need help.

multimedia	multicultural	composure	confide
multilingual	compatible	multipurpose	conjecture

1. The two friends were so _____ that they could work together on any project.

2. They tried to find some solid facts to back up their _____

3. The student showed great _____ as she stood in front of the class delivering her campaign speech.

4. A good friend is one you can _____ in knowing that your secret will be safe.

5. Last spring, our class created a _____ presentation for the entire school, and I was featured in one of the videos.

6. It's best to use a _____ cleaner if you have a messy house but very little time to clean it.

7. Every year our city has a _____ festival, and people from all over the world are invited.

8. The professor is _____ , but he prefers to speak Spanish.

THE RANSOM OF RED CHIEF

THE RANSOM OF RED CHIEF

Reading Check

Directions: Recall all characters and events in the story. Then answer each question in sentences or phrases.

1. What is the first clue that the kidnapping might not turn out as Bill and Sam planned?

_____

_____

_____

2. Describe Red Chief.

_____

_____

_____

3. How does Red Chief feel about being kidnapped?

_____

_____

_____

4. Who is in charge of the situation at the cave? Explain?

_____

_____

_____

5. Why does Mr. Dorset ask the kidnappers for money?

_____

_____

_____

THE RANSOM OF RED CHIEF

THE RANSOM OF RED CHIEF

Question Support

TEXT ANALYSIS

For questions 1–3, see page 63 of the Student Edition.

Directions: Answer each question.

4. Predict Two things the kidnappers did not anticipate were the following:

_____

_____

_____

5. Analyze Conflict and Resolution Decide which of the following outcomes is ironic. Then underline a choice in parentheses and complete the sentence.
a. Kidnappers take a young boy. The boy sneaks away at night and returns home.
b. A boy is kidnapped. The ransom is paid, the boy is released, and the kidnappers are arrested by the police.
c. A boy is missing. His parents call the police. A search is organized to find the boy.
d. A boy is kidnapped. The kidnappers are threatened and abused by the boy.

Outcome (a, b, c, d) is ironic because _____

_____

_____

6. Draw Conclusions

Why do you think O. Henry has Sam use words like "apparition," "undeleterious,"

"fraudulent," and "philoprogenitiveness" at the beginning of the story? _____

_____

_____

Underline one choice in parentheses and then complete the following sentence.

I (do, don't) think Sam and Bill have been successful in their previous schemes because

_____

_____

THE RANSOM OF RED CHIEF

THE RANSOM OF RED CHIEF

Grammar in Context

AVOID RUN-ON SENTENCES

A **run-on sentence** is two or more sentences written as though they were a single sentence. To correct a run-on sentence, you can

- insert an end mark and start a new sentence
- insert a comma and a coordinating conjunction, such as *and, but, or,* or *so*
- change the comma to a semicolon

  Original: The men were surprised, they didn't expect the boy to be so much trouble.
  Revised: The men were surprised. They didn't expect the boy to be so much trouble.

Directions: Rewrite the following sentences so that they are no longer run-ons.

1. They thought the boy would be afraid, he actually liked being kidnapped.

   _____

   _____

2. The boy threw rocks at them, he was more trouble than he was worth.

   _____

   _____

3. Bill was afraid of being left alone with the boy, he wasn't sure what the boy would do.

   _____

   _____

4. They thought the boy's father would pay them a ransom it turned out that they were the ones who had to pay.

   _____

   _____

5. The crooks ran away from the boy's house as fast as they could, they were afraid the boy would run after them.

   _____

   _____

Reading Fluency

COPY MASTER

TRACKING ORAL READING RATE AND ACCURACY

Directions: "The Ransom of Red Chief" tells the story of a young boy who outsmarts his kidnappers. Use this passage from the story with the activity on page 52. Follow the directions on that page.

We selected for our victim the only child of a prominent citizen named Ebenezer Dorset. The father was respectable and tight, a mortgage fancier and a stern, upright collection-plate passer and forecloser. The kid was a boy of ten, with bas-relief freckles, and hair the color of the cover of the magazine you buy at the news-stand when you want to catch a train. Bill and me figured that Ebenezer would melt down for a ransom of two thousand dollars to a cent. But wait till I tell you.

About two miles from Summit was a little mountain, covered with a dense cedar brake. On the rear elevation of this mountain was a cave. There we stored provisions.

One evening after sundown, we drove in a buggy past old Dorset's house. The kid was in the street, throwing rocks at a kitten on the opposite fence.

"Hey, little boy!" says Bill, "would you like to have a bag of candy and a nice ride?"

The boy catches Bill neatly in the eye with a piece of brick.

"That will cost the old man an extra five hundred dollars," says Bill, climbing over the wheel. (194 words)

—O. Henry, from "The Ransom of Red Chief"

THE RANSOM OF RED CHIEF

THE RANSOM OF RED CHIEF   COPY MASTER

Reading Fluency

TRACKING ORAL READING RATE AND ACCURACY

When you read aloud, your goal is to help the listener understand the text. To do this, read the words accurately and with expression. Use a normal speaking rate.

Directions to the Reader:

- Use this page with the passage on page 51. Read the passage in a natural tone of voice to your partner for one minute. He or she will tell you when to start and stop.
- Read the same passage three more times. Your goal is to increase your speed each time, while still reading each word accurately.
- Your partner will calculate your score, which shows how you compare to others at your grade level. Answer the questions below the chart to evaluate your progress.

Directions to the Checker:

- Tell your partner when to begin reading. As your partner reads, follow along. Lightly underline each word your partner skips or mispronounces. Jot down words he or she adds.
- After one minute, say "stop" and circle the last word your partner read. Share the marks you made with your partner.
- To calculate the reading fluency score, subtract the number of errors your partner made from the number of words read in a minute. Count as an error any words your partner left out, added, or mispronounced. If your partner substituted one word for another (*home*, for example), that substitution counts as an error as well. Put a checkmark in the table to show the reading score.
- Then erase the marks on the passage and tell your partner to begin again.

Reading 4											
Reading 3											
Reading 2											
Reading 1											
Number of Words Read Correctly Per Minute	1–77 10th Percentile	78–98 20th Percentile	99–106 25th Percentile	107–112 30th Percentile	113–124 40th Percentile	125–133 50th Percentile	134–145 60th Percentile	146–155 70th Percentile	156–161 75th Percentile	162–168 80th Percentile	169–185 90th Percentile

Directions: Write your answer to the following questions on the back of this sheet.

1. How did reading the passage several times affect your speed and accuracy?

2. Summarize the effect of repeated readings on your understanding of the passage.

THE RANSOM OF RED CHIEF

Clean Sweep

Joan Bauer

WHY THIS SELECTION?

In this contemporary short story, Joan Bauer creates a relevant narrator who speaks to the students in their language while still portraying qualities that make her a strong role model.

ABOUT THIS SELECTION

Student/Teacher's Edition Pages: 66–79
Difficulty Level: Average
Readability Scores: Lexile: 950; Fry: 9; Dale-Chall: 6.5

Summary Katie has been working in her mother's cleaning business since her father died and left the family without any money. She still grieves for him. While cleaning out Mrs. Leonardo's attic, she finds an old children's book, the cause of a breach between Mrs. Leonardo and her sister. Through Katie's efforts, Mrs. Leonardo effects a reconciliation, and Katie learns that memories are powerful and precious.

Engaging the Students This story offers students an opportunity to explore the key idea of treasure. The narrator and Mrs. Leonardo both discover that memory-provoking items are precious. As students read the story, they are challenged to think about what they consider to be treasures and why.

COMMON CORE STANDARDS FOCUS

- Conflicts and Subplots
- Sequence

LESSON RESOURCES

Plan and Teach

Student Copy Masters

ⓘ Lesson resources are also available on the **Teacher One Stop DVD-ROM** and online at <u>thinkcentral.com</u>.

CLEAN SWEEP

Lesson Plan and Resource Guide

Clean Sweep
Short Story by Joan Bauer

Common Core Focus

RL 3 Analyze how dialogue or incidents in a story propel the action. **RL 5** Analyze how the structure of text contributes to its meaning. **W 2b** Use dialogue to develop characters. **L 1** Demonstrate command of standard English grammar when writing. **L 6** Use accurately grade-appropriate words.

Unless otherwise noted, all resources can be found in the *Resource Manager*.
ⓘ Lesson resources are also available on the **Teacher One Stop DVD-ROM** and online at **thinkcentral.com.** The Student Edition and selected copy masters are available electronically on the ⬛ **Student One Stop DVD-ROM.**

Student/Teacher's Edition Pages	Additional Resources CM = Copy Master T = Transparency
Focus and Motivate	
❏ Big Question p. 66	❏ ⓘ **PowerNotes DVD-ROM** and online at **thinkcentral.com**
❏ Author Biography p. 67	❏ ⓘ Literature and Reading Center at **thinkcentral.com**
Teach	
❏ Internal and External Conflict p. 67	❏ ⓘ **PowerNotes DVD-ROM** and online at **thinkcentral.com**
❏ Sequence p. 67	❏ Sequence CM— English p. 65, Spanish p. 66 ⓓ ❏ ⓘ **PowerNotes DVD-ROM** and online at **thinkcentral.com**
❏ Vocabulary in Context p. 67	❏ Vocabulary Study CM p. 67 ⓓ ❏ ⓘ **PowerNotes DVD-ROM** and online at **thinkcentral.com**

ⓓ = Resources for Differentiation

CLEAN SWEEP

Student/Teacher's Edition Pages	Additional Resources CM = Copy Master T = Transparency
Practice and Apply: Guided Practice	
Selection and Teacher Notes ❑ "Clean Sweep," pp. 68–76	❑ 🖫 **Audio Anthology CD** Ⅾ ❑ Summary CM—English and Spanish p. 61, Haitian Creole and Vietnamese p. 62 Ⅾ ❑ Reading Fluency CM p. 73 ❑ 🧰 **Best Practices Toolkit** ❑ Read Aloud/Think Aloud p. A34 [T] Ⅾ ❑ ❶ ThinkAloud Models at **thinkcentral.com** ❑ ❶ Audio Summaries at **thinkcentral.com**
Practice and Apply: After Reading	
❑ Selection Questions p. 77	❑ Reading Check CM p. 70 ❑ Conflicts and Subplots CM— English p. 63, Spanish p. 64 Ⅾ ❑ Question Support CM p. 71 Ⅾ ❑ Additional Selection Questions p. 57 Ⅾ ❑ Ideas for Extension p. 58 Ⅾ
❑ Vocabulary Practice p. 74 ❑ Academic Vocabulary in Writing p. 74 ❑ Vocabulary Strategy: Suffixes That Form Nouns p. 74	❑ Vocabulary Practice CM p. 68 ❑ Academic Vocabulary CM p. 2 ❑ Additional Academic Vocabulary CM p. 3 ❑ Vocabulary Strategy CM p. 69 ❑ ❶ *WordSharp* Interactive Vocabulary Tutor CD-ROM and online at **thinkcentral.com**
❑ Grammar in Context p. 75 ❑ Writing Prompt p. 75	❑ Use Progressive Form Correctly CM p. 72 ❑ Grammar Handbook—Student Edition p. R46 ❑ ❶ GrammarNotes DVD-ROM at **thinkcentral.com** ❑ ❶ Interactive Revision Lessons on WriteSmart CD-ROM and online at **thinkcentral.com**

Ⅾ = Resources for Differentiation

Resource Manager

CLEAN SWEEP

Student/Teacher's Edition Pages	Additional Resources CM = Copy Master T = Transparency
Assess and Reteach	
Assess	❑ **Diagnostic and Selection Tests** ❑ Selection Tests A, B/C pp. 31–32, 33–34 D ❑ ℹ️ ThinkCentral Online Assessment ❑ 💿 ExamView Test Generator on the **Teacher One Stop DVD-ROM**

Reteach
 	
❑   Conflicts and Subplots
❑   Sequence
❑   Suffixes That Form Nouns
	❑ ℹ️ Level Up Online Tutorials on **thinkcentral.com**
	❑ ℹ️ Reteaching Worksheets on **thinkcentral.com**
	   ❑ Literature Lesson 6: Conflict
	   ❑ Literature Lesson 7: Flashbacks
	   ❑ Reading Lesson 6: Recognizing Sequence and Chronological Order
	   ❑ Vocabulary Lesson 5: Noun Suffixes

D = Resources for Differentiation

If you are following the *Essential Course of Study*, this selection may also be found in

- **Interactive Reader**
- **Adapted Interactive Reader**
- 💿 **Adapted Interactive Reader: Audio Tutor**
- **English Language Learner Adapted interactive Reader**

CLEAN SWEEP

Additional Selection Questions

Use to supplement the questions on SE page 77.

Differentiation Use these questions to provide customized practice with comprehension and critical thinking skills.

Easy

1. *When does trash become* **TREASURE?**
   What objects does Katie treasure because of their association with her father? (*She values his essays and photographs and the children's book from which he used to read bedtime stories.*)

2. **Identify Internal and External Conflict** Reread lines 89–102. What is Katie's internal conflict in these lines? What is the external conflict? (*Katie's internal conflict is over whether or not to keep arguing with Mrs. Leonardo, even though she is right. The external conflict is between Katie and Mrs. Leonardo, over whether or not to save the old tax forms.*)

Average

3. *When does trash become* **TREASURE?**
   Why is Katie able to help Mrs. Leonardo figure out what is important and what she should treasure? (*The loss of Katie's father taught her that caring for family members before it is too late is important and that memories are to be treasured. She is able to pass her wisdom on to Mrs. Leonardo indirectly through her questions and comments.*)

4. **Analyze Internal and External Conflict** Reread lines 146–150. How is the activity of Katie and her mother an attempt to solve an external and an internal conflict? (*The external conflict is imposing order on Katie's father's papers and belongings. By doing this, they are also struggling to come to terms with their loss and the disorder that his death has thrown their world into.*)

5. **Analyze Sequence** The sequence of events in the story proper does not start until line 49. What function do the first 48 lines serve? (*Lines 1–48 introduce the characters and the cleaning business that Katie's mother runs.*)

Challenging

6. *When does trash become* **TREASURE?**
   What might the author be saying about the relationship between organization and what is important in life? (*In order to recognize treasure, it is important to clear away the clutter of one's life. When someone's life gets too full of stuff, significant people and things can get lost.*)

7. **Evaluate Sequence** Why might the author choose to reveal the details about Katie's father in a flashback, rather than as part of the story's exposition? (*Keeping details unknown until later in the story enables readers to form their own impressions of the characters before being influenced by knowledge of the tragedies in their lives. Flashbacks also allow the author to create suspense.*)

Ideas for Extension

Differentiation These activities provide students with a variety of options for demonstrating understanding of lesson concepts.

EXPLORATIONS AND ACTIVITIES

AD CAMPAIGN: SUMMARIZE MAIN IDEAS

Discuss the ways in which Katie's mother already has a fairly effective client presentation and analyze the persuasive techniques she uses. Then ask students to imagine that she wants to attract more new customers by mounting a major ad campaign.

Assign small groups of students to work on different aspects of the campaign. Have one group write a jingle, another design a billboard, a third create print ads, and a fourth script a radio spot. Students should use what the story tells them about the Clean Sweep cleaning service as the basis for their factual information.

Have the groups present their components of the campaign. Discuss the methods of persuasion used in each and why each is effective.

STORY MAP: EXPLORE CHARACTER AND PLOT

Point out to students that the organization of the story has potential for further development. The story of Katie and her family is the major plot, but each client that they work for has his or her own story, just as Mrs. Leonardo did.

Have students work in small groups to complete a story map for another subplot. They might begin by brainstorming the kinds of characters that Katie might work for and the reasons they might need their houses organized. Remind students to develop a central conflict.

After students have presented their completed story maps to the class, discuss the concept of a frame story and how it applies to "Clean Sweep," as well as the scope that it allows an author.

Pre-AP Challenge: Have students write the stories they have mapped. Then ask them to weave their stories into the framework plot. They will need to extend the story of Katie and her family further to act as a bridge for the new subplot. Have students read what they have written to the class.

SHOW AND TELL: EXAMINE KEY CONCEPT

Discuss how this story brings out the importance of recognizing treasure in one's life, whether it is another person or an object.

Ask students to select an item that is a treasure in their lives. They might choose the object that they examined in the web on page 62 or something else. Have students organize and give a short presentation about why the object is important to them.

CLEAN SWEEP

COMPARISON MATRIX: COMPARE AND CONTRAST CHARACTERS

Point out that the stories in this unit so far have had first-person narrators. Sometimes, details about the character of the narrator are given directly; most of the time, readers make inferences based on what the narrator says and does.

Ask students to think about Squeaky, the narrator in "Raymond's Run," and the ways in which she is similar to and different from Katie, the narrator in this story. For example, both girls are responsible for brothers, although in different ways. Both are honest about their feelings and have strong opinions.

Divide students into small groups to compare Katie to a first-person narrator of their choice. Ask them to organize their comparison in a matrix or other chart. Students should use their charts to support their opinions in a class discussion.

INQUIRY AND RESEARCH

CLEANING PRODUCTS

Tell students that some cleaning products can be quite damaging to the environment. Many companies, however, market environmentally safe cleaning agents that are supposed to do as good a job as traditional products.

Ask groups of students to research environmentally safe cleaning substances and prepare an oral consumer report on a specific class of cleanser, such as dishwashing soaps or bathroom disinfectants. Students should use print and electronic resources to find out about these products.

Have groups present their reports to the class. Discuss what students learned from doing their research.

WRITING

EXAMINE CONFLICT: ADVICE COLUMN

Have students work in pairs. Ask one partner to compose a letter that Katie might have written to an advice columnist, explaining the many demands on her time and asking for ideas about how to ease her stressful life. Then have the other partner respond to this letter with solutions for some of Katie's conflicts.

ANALYZE CHARACTER: SKETCH

Although Katie's mother plays a minor role in the story, what Katie reveals about her words and actions helps to give readers an understanding of her traits. Have students write a description or sketch of Katie's mother, supporting their inferences about her character with details from the story.

EXPLORE KEY IDEA: INVITATION

Suppose Mrs. Leonardo wrote a note to invite her sister to dinner. What might she have said? Ask students to write the invitation, keeping in mind the circumstances that led up to it. Have students maintain Mrs. Leonardo's perspective throughout.

CLEAN SWEEP

Teacher Notes

Review and Evaluate Outcome
What did I want students to know or be able to do?
How successful was the lesson?

Evaluate Process
What worked? • Strategies • Resources • Differentiation What did not work? Why not?

Reflect
The next time I teach "Clean Sweep," what will I do differently? Why?

Plan Ahead
What must I do next?

CLEAN SWEEP

Summary

CLEAN SWEEP

Joan Bauer
Setting: The suburbs, present day

When Katie's father dies suddenly leaving his family with no insurance money to pay the bills, Katie's life is thrown into turmoil. There is no time to mourn his death, for the whole family is forced to find a way to support themselves. Katie's mom starts a cleaning service called Clean Sweep, and Katie and her brother Benjamin are expected to help after school. Today Katie has a big job to do—packing up Mrs. Leonardo's attic.

Mrs. Leonardo is a lonely old widow who claims that everyone in her family has deserted her. As they clean, Mrs. Leonardo tells Katie stories about her life. Mrs. Leonardo seems sad as she holds up a lace tablecloth that she got as a wedding gift and used only once—for her twenty-fifth anniversary. Katie suggests that she could start using the tablecloth again, but Mrs. Leonardo replies that there is no one she would invite to dinner. Then, Mrs. Leonardo finds a book she thought she had given to her sister years ago. Katie urges Mrs. Leonard to call her sister and tell her about the book, but Mrs. Leonardo tells Katie to leave. When Katie returns, the house smells of good food and Mrs. Leonardo asks Katie to get the lace tablecloth and the book from the trunk.

CAMBIO TOTAL

Joan Bauer
Escenario: Los suburbios, época actual

Cuando el padre de Katie muere repentinamente dejando a su familia sin un seguro para pagar las cuentas, la vida de Katie se vuelve turbulenta. No hay tiempo para acongojarse por su muerte, ya que toda la familia se ve forzada a encontrar una manera de mantenerse a ellos mismos. La mamá de Katie inicia un servicio de limpieza llamado Cambio total, y Katie y su hermano Benjamín tienen que ayudar después de la escuela. Hoy Katie tiene un trabajo importante: recoger el ático de la Sra. Leonardo.

La Sra. Leonardo es una mujer anciana, viuda y sola, quien dice que toda su familia la ha abandonado. Mientras limpian, la Sra. Leonardo le cuenta a Katie historias sobre su vida. La Sra. Leonardo se ve triste mientras sostiene un mantel de encaje que recibió como regalo de bodas y sólo se usó una vez para su aniversario número veinticinco. Katie le insinúa que podría usar de nuevo el mantel, pero la Sra. Leonardo le responde que no hay nadie a quien ella invitaría a cenar. Después, la Sra. Leonardo se encuentra un libro que pensaba que se lo había dado a su hermana hacía años. Katie incita a la Sra. Leonardo a que llame a su hermana y que le mencione el libro, pero la Sra. Leonardo le dice a Katie que se vaya. Cuando Katie regresa, la casa huele a comida sabrosa y la Sra. Leonardo le pide a Katie que traiga el mantel de encaje y el libro del baúl.

CLEAN SWEEP

Summary

CLEAN SWEEP

Joan Bauer

Espas ak tan: Fobou yo, tan kounye a

Lè papa Kati mouri toudenkou etan l kite fanmi li san lajan asirans pou peye bòdwo yo, Kati vin gen anpil pwoblèm nan lavi li. Pa gen tan pou kriye lanmò li, paske tout fanmi an fòse jwenn yon fason pou sipòte tèt yo. Manman Kati kòmanse yon sèvis netwayaj ki rele Clean Sweep, epi yo mande Kati ak frè li a, Benjamen, pou yo bay èd apre lekòl. Jodi a Kati jwenn yon gwo djòb pou li fè—anpile bagay nan galta Madan Lewonado.

Madan Lewonado se yon vèv k ap viv poukont li epi ki fè konnen tout moun nan fanmi li kite li. Pandan y ap netwaye, Madan Lewonado rakonte Kati istwa sou lavi li. Madan Lewonado parèt tris, pandan li kenbe yon nap ki gen dantèl, li te resevwa kòm kado maryaj epi li te itilize li sèlman yon fwa—pou vennsenkyèm anivèsè li. Kati sijere li ka kòmanse itilize nap la ankò, men Madan Lewonado di li pa genyen pèsòn pou li envite vin dine lakay li. Apre sa, Madan Lewonado jwenn yon liv li panse li te bay sè li depi anpil ane. Kati ankouraje Madan Lewonado pou rele sè li a epi pou li pale ak li osijè liv la ki la, men Madan Leonardo mande Kati pou li ale. Lè Katie retounen, lip ran yon bon sant manje nan kay la epi Madan Lewonado mande Kati pou li pran nap ki gen dantèl la ak liv la nan mal la. .

Quét Sạch

Joan Bauer

Bối cảnh: Khu vực ngoại ô, thời hiện tại

Khi cha của Katie chết bất ngờ để lại gia đình ông không có tiền bảo hiểm để trả các hóa đơn, cuộc sống của Katie rơi vào trình trạng hỗn độn. Không có thời gian để thương tiếc về cái chết của ông, cả gia đình buộc phải tìm cách để tự nuôi sống mình. Mẹ Katie bắt đầu làm dịch vụ vệ sinh, gọi là Quét Sạch, còn Katie và người anh em trai cô là Benjamin thì trông đợi phụ việc sau giờ học. Hôm nay Katie có một việc lớn phải làm—thu dọn gác mái của bà Leonardo.

Bà Leonardo là một quả phụ già cô đơn, bà than phiền rằng mọi người trong gia đình bà đã rời bỏ bà. Khi họ dọn dẹp, bà Leonardo kể cho Katie các câu chuyện về cuộc đời bà. Bà Leonardo tỏ ra buồn bã khi bà giơ một chiếc khăn trải bàn bằng ren lên, đó là món quà cưới của bà và bà chỉ dùng có một lần—ngày kỷ niệm 25 năm cưới của bà. Katie đề nghị rằng bà Leonardo có thể bắt đầu dùng lại chiếc khăn bàn, nhưng bà Leonardo trả lời rằng bà không có ai để mời đến ăn tối cả. Sau đó bà Leonardo tìm thấy một cuốn sách mà bà nghĩ bà đã đưa cho người chị em gái của bà nhiều năm trước đây. Katie giục bà Leonard gọi điện cho người chị em của bà để nói về cuốn sách, nhưng bà Leonardo bảo Katie đi về. Khi Katie trở lại, trong nhà bốc mùi thức ăn ngon và bà Leonardo bảo Katie lấy chiếc khăn bàn ren và cuốn sách từ trong hòm ra.

CLEAN SWEEP

Text Analysis

CONFLICTS AND SUBPLOTS

A **conflict** is a struggle between opposing forces that creates the tension or suspense in a story or play. There are two types of conflict:

- **External conflict** is a struggle between a character and an outside force.
- **Internal conflict** is a struggle within a character's mind.

Directions: In the chart show how a past event causes internal and external conflict. An example has been done for you.

Event	External Conflicts	Internal Conflicts
Father dies suddenly	Mother needs to find way to pay bills	

CLEAN SWEEP

CAMBIO TOTAL

Text Analysis

CONFLICTS AND SUBPLOTS

Un **conflicto** es una lucha entre fuerzas opuestas que crean tensión o suspenso en un relato o en una obra. Hay dos tipos de conflicto.

- **Conflicto externo** es la lucha entre un personaje y una fuerza externa.
- **Conflicto interno** es la lucha dentro de la mente del personaje.

Instrucciones: Muestra en la gráfica cómo un acontecimiento anterior causa un conflicto interno y externo. Sigue el ejemplo.

Acontecimiento	Conflictos externos	Conflictos internos
El padre muere repentinamente.	La madre necesita encontrar una manera de pagar las cuentas.	

SPANISH

CLEAN SWEEP
Reading Skill

SEQUENCE

To fully understand a story, you must recognize the **sequence,** or order, of the events described. While events are often presented in the order in which they occur, sometimes the action is interrupted to present a **flashback,** or scene from an earlier time, to help explain a character's actions.

Directions: As you read "Clean Sweep," keep track of the sequence by recording important events in the sequence chart.

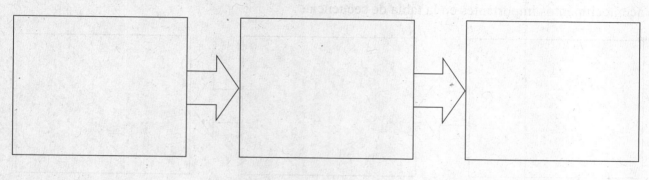

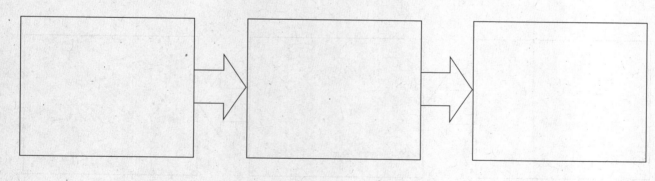

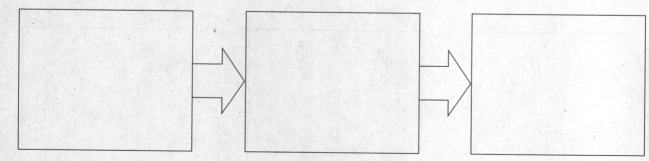

CLEAN SWEEP

CAMBIO TOTAL

Reading Skill

SEQUENCE

Para entender un relato completamente, debes reconocer la **secuencia,** u orden, de los acontecimientos descritos. Aunque los acontecimientos frecuentemente se presentan en el orden en el cual ocurren, algunas veces la acción se ve interrumpida para presentar un **retroceso al pasado,** o escena de una época anterior, para explicar las acciones del personaje.

Instrucciones: Mientras lees "Cambio total", sigue la secuencia anotando acontecimientos importantes en la tabla de secuencia.

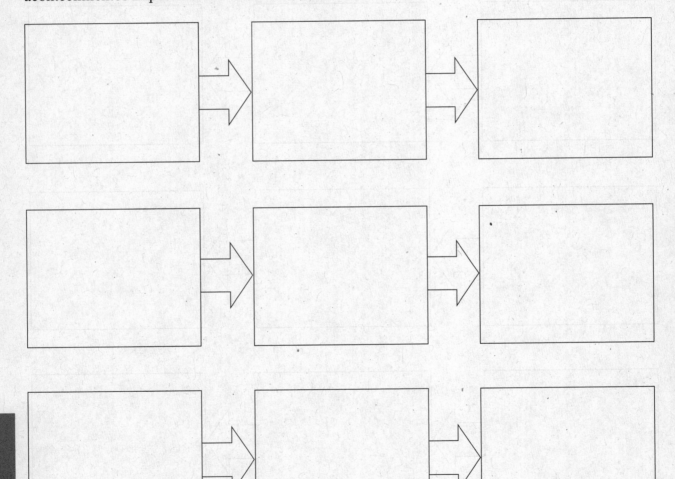

SPANISH

CLEAN SWEEP

Vocabulary Study

VOCABULARY IN CONTEXT

A. Directions: As your teacher reads each sentence, listen for the boldfaced word and clues to its meaning. Together discuss possible meanings of the word.

1. Benjamin's decision to help with today's job is an **aberration.** He usually avoids work.

2. Fingerprints on the woodwork and stacks of yellowing newspapers on the floor made the apartment appear **dingy.**

3. The customer lost a **miniscule** diamond chip from her ring and demanded that we sift through the vacuum cleaner bag to try to find it.

4. Clients trust the cleaners completely. To maintain the relationship, the employees need to act with **propriety** at all times.

5. She was in **turmoil** over whether to accept the unpleasant job or give up the money she needed.

6. The **vileness** of the moldy carpet's odor was even more unbearable after we ripped up the carpet.

B. Directions: Use the boldfaced words from Part A to answer each question. Be prepared to give reasons for your answers.

1. Which words could be used in relationship to behavior?

   _____

   _____

2. Which words describe a mental condition or physical appearance?

   _____

   _____

3. Which words have negative meanings and connotations?

   _____

   _____

CLEAN SWEEP

CLEAN SWEEP   COPY MASTER

Vocabulary Practice

| dingy | miniscule | propriety | turmoil | vileness | aberration |

A. Directions: Write the word from the box that correctly completes each sentence.

1. The well-kept house was an _____ compared to the filthy homes Katie usually cleaned.

2. She had no idea why the family hired her to clean, as there seemed to be a _____ amount of dust and dirt.

3. The walls were a little _____ but Katie knew that they would clean easily.

4. The _____ of the ugly dust mite would surely scare some customers.

5. Customers who saw these ugly creatures would lose all sense of _____ and let out a shriek as they ran for the door.

6. Her father's sudden death threw Katie's whole world into _____; it seemed that nothing would ever be the same.

B. Directions: Circle the word in each group that has the opposite meaning of the boldfaced word.

7. **dingy**
   a. curved   c. quiet
   b. angry   d. bright

8. **miniscule**
   a. significant   c. useless
   b. personal   d. special

9. **propriety**
   a. success   c. honesty
   b. rudeness   d. sequence

10. **turmoil**
   a. appearance   c. distinction
   b. calm   d. astonishment

11. **vileness**
   a. backwardness   c. difficulty
   b. pleasantness   d. withered

12. **aberration**
   a. consistency   c. assumption
   b. enthusiasm   d. discussion

CLEAN SWEEP

CLEAN SWEEP

Vocabulary Strategy

SUFFIXES THAT FORM NOUNS

A suffix is a word part that appears at the end of a root or base word to form a new word. Some suffixes, such as those in the vocabulary words *vileness* and *aberration,* can be added to words to form nouns. Knowing that the suffixes in the following box all mean "state, condition, quality, or act of" can help you determine the meaning of many words.

-ence	-ity	-ness	-ment	-tion

A. Directions: For each sentence, write the base word and suffix in the boldfaced word. Then define the noun that has been made by adding the suffix.

1. With high heat and humidity, there is a strong **possibility** of thundershowers.

   _____

2. The appearance of a funnel cloud is an **indication** that a tornado is approaching.

   _____

3. The stage was set, the lights dimmed, and the performers took their places in **readiness** for the opening act of the school play.

   _____

4. They were surprised at her **persistence** as she refused to give up until the last piece of the puzzle was in place.

   _____

B. Directions: Write the word from the box that best completes each sentence.

appointment	scarcity	independence	meditation

1. Children tiptoed past the door, reluctant to interrupt her _____.

2. The severe drought resulted in a _____ of food supplies.

3. The teenagers looked forward to learning to drive and gaining _____.

4. They eagerly awaited the _____ of a new coach for the team.

CLEAN SWEEP

CLEAN SWEEP

Reading Check

Directions: Recall the events in Joan Bauer's short story. Then answer the questions in phrases or sentences.

1. What do Katie and her mother do to make money?

_____

_____

_____

2. How does Katie feel about Mrs. Leonardo at first?

_____

_____

_____

3. What has happened to Katie's father?

_____

_____

_____

4. What does Mrs. Leonardo say is the reason that her sister wanted the storybook?

_____

_____

_____

5. What is Mrs. Leonardo preparing for at the end of the story?

_____

_____

_____

CLEAN SWEEP

CLEAN SWEEP

Question Support

TEXT ANALYSIS

For questions 1–3, see page 77 of the Student Edition.

Directions: Answer each question.

4. **Identify Sequence** Underline the information that is revealed about Katie in a flashback.

   a. She resents her brother's behavior

   b. She thinks Mrs. Leonardo is mean

   c. Her father died suddenly

   d. She is good at cleaning teenage bedrooms.

   e. She was afraid they would loose their house.

   f. She regrets not making her father breakfast.

5. **Examine Conflicts** In the chart, record two conflicts Katie faced when her father died and tell how each one was resolved.

Conflict	Resolution

6. **Analyze Character Motivations** Complete the following sentence.

   I think Mrs. Leonardo decided to reconnect with her sister because _____

   _____

7. **Analyze Subplot** A **subplot** is a minor plot that involves another conflict in the story.

   What is Mrs. Leonardo's conflict with her sister? _____

   _____

   How is this conflict resolved? _____

   _____

8. **Make Judgments** Choose one word in parentheses and then complete the following sentence.

   Katie's brother (is, isn't) a hypochondriac because _____

   _____

CLEAN SWEEP

CLEAN SWEEP   COPY MASTER

Grammar in Context

USE PROGRESSIVE FORM CORRECTLY

When you are writing about an event that's in progress, use the **progressive form** of a verb. The progressive form is made by using the same tense of the verb *to be* with the present participle, which is formed by using the verb stem and adding *ing*.

Example: She **is cleaning** the attic. (The cleaning is an ongoing action.)

Tenses	Examples
1. Present Progressive	*We are laughing.*
2. Past Progressive	*We were laughing.*
3. Future Progressive	*We will be laughing.*
4. Present Perfect Progressive	*We have been laughing.*
5. Past Perfect Progressive	*We had been laughing.*
6. Future Perfect Progressive	*We will have been laughing*

Directions: Choose one of the verbs below to write six sentences each using a different progressive tense.

conclude	imply	perform

1. Present Progressive: _____

_____

2. Past Progressive: _____

_____

3. Future Progressive: _____

_____

4. Present Perfect Progressive: _____

_____

5. Past Perfect Progressive: _____

_____

6. Future Perfect Progressive: _____

CLEAN SWEEP

Reading Fluency

PHRASING

One key to better fluency is proper **phrasing,** or using pauses to group words into meaningful chunks. To improve your phrasing, look for commas, semicolons, periods and other punctuation marks as you read. These marks often hint at natural places to pause, take a breath, or come to a complete stop.

A. Directions: Read silently this passage from *Great Expectations*. In it, a young boy named Pip describes an eccentric character named Miss Havisham. The slash marks indicate natural places to stop or take a breath. Then practice reading the passage aloud.

But, / I saw that everything within my view which ought to be white, / had been white long ago, / and had lost its luster, / and was faded and yellow. I saw that the bride within the bridal dress / had withered like the dress, / and like the flowers, / and had no brightness left / but the brightness of her sunken eyes. . . .

B. Directions: Draw slash marks in another passage from the story to show where you might stop or pause to take a breath. Practice reading the passage, and then read it to your partner. Ask your partner if your phrasing seems natural.

"Who is it?" said the lady at the table.

"Pip, ma'am."

"Pip?"

"Mr. Pumblechook's boy, ma'am. Come—to play."

"Come nearer; let me look at you. Come close."

It was when I stood before her, avoiding her eyes, that I took

note of the surrounding objects in detail, and saw that her watch

had stopped at twenty minutes to nine, and that a clock in the

room had stopped at twenty minutes to nine.

"Look at me," said Miss Havisham. "You are not afraid of a

woman who has never seen the sun since you were born?"

READING FLUENCY CONTINUED

I regret to state that I was not afraid of telling the enormous

lie comprehended in the answer "No."

"Do you know what I touch here?" she said, laying her hands,

one upon the other, on her left side.

"Yes, ma'am." . . .

"What do I touch?"

"Your heart."

"Broken!"

—Charles Dickens, from *Great Expectations*

Essential Course of Study ECOS **Lesson at a Glance**

The Tell-Tale Heart

Edgar Allan Poe

WHY THIS SELECTION?

This classic tale of horror introduces students to one of the best-known works of Edgar Allan Poe and provides an excellent example of the "unreliable narrator." It lets students examine the way an author creates suspense.

ABOUT THIS SELECTION

Student/Teacher's Edition Pages: 80–89
Difficulty Level: Challenging
Readability Scores: Lexile: 850; Fry: 5; Dale-Chall: 6.4

Summary The narrator describes how he became obsessed by the idea of killing an old man. Throughout the murder, he focuses on the beating of the old man's heart. Then he hides his victim's body. When the police arrive, the narrator hears a pounding sound that grows louder and louder. Convinced that the sound is the old man's heart, the tormented narrator confesses his crime.

Engaging the Students This story offers students an opportunity to explore the key idea of suspicion. The narrator is extremely mistrustful, and his suspicions prompt him to plot the murder of an old man. As students read the story and evaluate the narrator, they can reflect on the signs that arouse suspicion.

COMMON CORE STANDARDS FOCUS

- Suspense
- Evaluate Narrator

LESSON RESOURCES

Plan and Teach

Student Copy Masters

ⓘ Lesson resources are also available on the **Teacher One Stop DVD-ROM** and online at <u>thinkcentral.com</u>.

Lesson Plan and Resource Guide

The Tell-Tale Heart
Short Story by Edgar Allan Poe

Common Core Focus

RL 4 Analyze the impact of word choices on meaning and tone. **RL 6** Analyze how differences in the points of view of the characters and the reader (e.g., created through the use of dramatic irony) create suspense. **L 4c** Consult reference materials (e.g., dictionaries, thesauruses) to determine [a word's] precise meaning.

Unless otherwise noted, all resources can be found in the *Resource Manager*.
❶ Lesson resources are also available on the **Teacher One Stop DVD-ROM** and online at **thinkcentral.com**. The Student Edition and selected copy masters are available electronically on the 💿 **Student One Stop DVD-ROM.**

Student/Teacher's Edition Pages	Additional Resources CM = Copy Master　T = Transparency
Focus and Motivate	
❑　Big Question p. 80	❑　❶ **PowerNotes DVD-ROM** and online at **thinkcentral.com**
❑　Author Biography p. 81	❑　❶ Literature and Reading Center at **thinkcentral.com**
Teach	
❑　Suspense p. 81	❑　❶ **PowerNotes DVD-ROM** and online at **thinkcentral.com**
❑　Evaluate Narrator p. 81	❑　Evaluate Narrator CM— English p. 87, Spanish p. 88 🄳
❑　Vocabulary in Context p. 81	❑　Vocabulary Study CM p. 89 🄳
	❑　❶ **PowerNotes DVD-ROM** and online at **thinkcentral.com**
Practice and Apply: Guided Practice	
Selection and Teacher Notes	❑　💿 **Audio Anthology CD** 🄳
❑　"The Tell–Tale Heart," pp. 82–87	❑　Summary CM—English and Spanish p. 83, Haitian Creole and Vietnamese p. 84 🄳
	❑　Reading Fluency CM p. 94
	❑　📦 **Best Practices Toolkit**
	❑　Two-Column Chart p. A25 [T] 🄳

🄳 = Resources for Differentiation

Student/Teacher's Edition Pages	Additional Resources CM = Copy Master T = Transparency
Practice and Apply: After Reading	
❑ Selection Questions p. 88	❑ Reading Check CM p. 92 ❑ Suspense CM—p. 85, Spanish p. 86 **D** ❑ Question Support CM p. 93 **D** ❑ Additional Selection Questions p. 78 **D** ❑ Ideas for Extension p. 79 **D**
❑ Vocabulary Practice p. 89 ❑ Academic Vocabulary in Writing p. 89 ❑ Vocabulary Strategy: Using Reference Aids p. 89	❑ Vocabulary Practice CM p. 90 ❑ Academic Vocabulary CM p. 2 ❑ Additional Academic Vocabulary CM p. 3 ❑ Vocabulary Strategy CM p. 91 ❑ ❶ *WordSharp* Interactive Vocabulary Tutor CD-ROM and online at **thinkcentral.com**
Assess and Reteach	
Assess	❑ **Diagnostic and Selection Tests** ❑ Selection Tests A, B/C pp. 35–36, 37–38 **D** ❑ ❶ ThinkCentral Online Assessment ❑ ✏ ExamView Test Generator on the **Teacher One Stop DVD-ROM**

Reteach
 ❑ Suspense
 ❑ Evaluate Narrator
 ❑ Using Reference Aids
	❑ ❶ Level Up Online Tutorials on **thinkcentral.com**
	 ❑ ❶ Reteaching Worksheets on **thinkcentral.com**
	   ❑ Literature Lesson 8: Foreshadowing and Suspense
	   ❑ Literature Lesson 10: Narrator
	   ❑ Vocabulary Lesson 24: Using Dictionaries and Glossaries

D = Resources for Differentiation

If you are following the *Essential Course of Study*, this selection may also be found in

- **Interactive Reader**
- **Adapted Interactive Reader**
- ✏ **Adapted Interactive Reader: Audio Tutor**
- **English Language Learner Adapted interactive Reader**

**Use to supplement the
questions on SE page 88.**

Differentiation Use these questions to provide customized practice with
comprehension and critical thinking skills.

Easy

1. *What makes you* **SUSPICIOUS?**
   Why does the narrator conclude that the old man doesn't suspect him of spying?
   (*The narrator thinks the old man is asleep.*)

2. **Evaluate Narrator** Do you believe the narrator when he says that he can hear
   the old man's heart, even after the murder? What other explanations can you
   think of? (*It is unlikely that the old man's heart is still beating. Therefore, the
   narrator might be hearing the beating of his own heart.*)

3. **Analyze Suspense** How does the first sentence of the story build suspense?
   (*The reader wonders why the narrator is so nervous.*)

Average

4. **Evaluate Narrator** In the first paragraph, the narrator says he is not mad, but
   then refers to "the disease" that sharpened his senses. What disease does the
   narrator believe himself to have? Do you agree with his self-diagnosis? (*The
   narrator has heightened senses and agitation. He says he isn't insane, but it
   would seem that he suffers from some sort of mental illness.*)

5. **Analyze Suspense** Poe uses foreshadowing throughout "The Tell–Tale Heart."
   He builds suspense by hinting about events that will happen later in the story.
   What details create foreshadowing in lines 1–16? (*The narrator mentions the
   disease, his notion of killing the old man, and the execution of his plan.*)

Challenging

6. *What makes you* **SUSPICIOUS?**
   According to the Key Idea paragraph on page 76, the narrator's suspicions lead
   to his downfall. Explain why this is the case. (*The narrator becomes obsessed
   with the notion that the old man is evil and eventually, this obsession leads
   him to commit a murder. Even after the old man is dead, the narrator remains
   suspicious and fearful. This fear leads him to confess to the crime.*)

7. **Evaluate Narrator** In "The Tell–Tale Heart," Poe's narrator uses first-person
   point of view. What are some possible reasons that Poe chose this technique?
   (*First-person point of view is more intimate; it allows the reader to get inside
   the mind of the narrator; it allows the reader to discover that the narrator is
   unbalanced, without the author stating this directly.*)

Ideas for Extension

Differentiation These activities provide students with a variety of options for demonstrating understanding of lesson concepts.

EXPLORATIONS AND ACTIVITIES

ILLUSTRATE TEXT: EXAMINE CHARACTER TRAITS

Poe provides no physical description of the narrator. A close reading reveals that this unnamed character is not identified as male or female. Ask students to create a portrait of the narrator. Students may choose any medium, including paint, charcoal, watercolors, or collage. Remind them that the appearance of this character is open to interpretation and that the illustrations in the selection are only one version of the events. Provide time for students to present and explain their portraits to the class.

PANTOMIME: INTERPRET PLOT

Have students select a passage of the text to interpret through pantomime. Encourage them to creep and move the way the narrator does. Assist students in selecting atmospheric instrumental music to accompany their movement.

LIST DETAILS: VISUALIZE DESCRIPTION

Read aloud a passage from the text and ask students to close their eyes as they visualize the characters, setting, and action. Ask students to list the details they recall. Then have them review the text to confirm their recollections.

VIEW FILM: COMPARE AND CONTRAST ELEMENTS OF FICTION

Show students a film adaptation of "The Tell–Tale Heart." Ask them to notice ways in which the film version deviates from the story. Have small groups of students discuss the differences and similarities between the story and the film adaptation. Lead the class in a discussion about the filmmaker's choices.

COURTROOM TRIAL: EXTEND PLOT

Stage the narrator's trial for murder. Select prosecuting and defense attorneys, witnesses, a defendant, and a judge. Remind students to use story details as they present and judge the case.

INQUIRY AND RESEARCH

FILM ADAPTATIONS

Since the silent movie era, filmmakers have made and remade movies of Poe's macabre tales. Have students work in pairs or triads to trace the history of films adapted from famous works of literature, using the Internet and library reference materials. Suggest that students organize the results of their research chronologically or by title. Provide time for students to report their findings to the class.

Pre-AP Challenge: Invite students to organize a Poe film festival. Have them obtain films of as many Poe stories as they can. Have them choose clips from the films and provide an introduction to each of the selections that gives adequate background and prepares the viewers for what they are to see. Then have students lead a class discussion afterwards, commenting on directors' interpretations of the stories and the versions they and the audience prefer.

WRITING

SUMMARIZE MAIN IDEAS AND DETAILS: POLICE REPORT

Ask students to imagine that they are the police officers called to investigate the scene of the crime. Have them write a police report of their investigation. Students should use details from the text as they report on the suspect, his behavior, the crime scene, and any evidence the officers might have discovered.

DEVELOP STORY ELEMENTS: MYSTERY STORY

Edgar Allan Poe is often cited as the father of the modern mystery story. Have students outline their own original mystery stories. Suggest that they begin by plotting the main characters (who), the setting (when and where), the mystery (what and how), and the motive (why). Once students have plotted these details, encourage them to complete their stories.

Teacher Notes

Review and Evaluate Outcome
What did I want students to know or be able to do?   How successful was the lesson?

Evaluate Process
What worked? • Strategies   • Resources   • Differentiation   What did not work? Why not?

Reflect
The next time I teach "The Tell–Tale Heart," what will I do differently? Why?

Plan Ahead
What must I do next?

Summary

THE TELL–TALE HEART

Edgar Allan Poe

Setting: A dark house, late at night

The narrator in this story begins by telling readers that he is not insane. However, readers must wonder if he is telling the truth. He begins to describe his grisly murder of an old man. He lives with the old man, and the old man's eye bothers him. The narrator compares the eye to a vulture's eye. Because the eye becomes more and more annoying to the narrator, he decides to kill the old man. He visits the old man's bedroom for seven nights in a row. On the eighth night, he kills him while the sound of the old man's heart beats loudly in his ears. He then hides the body under the floor. The police arrive to investigate. The narrator believes they will find nothing. Later, as he and the police talk, he begins to hear a muffled sound.

EL CORAZÓN DELATOR

Edgar Allan Poe

Escenario: Una casa obscura, altas horas de la noche

El narrador de esta historia comienza diciendo a los lectores que él no está demente. Sin embargo, los lectores deben preguntarse si él está diciendo la verdad. él comienza a describir su espantoso asesinato de un anciano. él vive con el anciano y el ojo del anciano le molesta. El narrador compara el ojo con el ojo de un buitre. Como el ojo se vuelve cada vez más molesto para el narrador, decide matar al anciano. Visita la habitación del anciano durante siete noches seguidas. Durante la octava noche, lo mata mientras el sonido del corazón del anciano golpea fuertemente sus oídos. Después oculta el cuerpo debajo del piso. La policía llega para investigar. El narrador cree que no van a encontrar nada. Más tarde, mientras él y la policía hablan, él comienza a escuchar un sonido amortiguado.

Summary

KÈ KI RAKONTE FAB LA

Edgar Allan Poe

Espas ak tan: Yon kay ki fènwa, ta lannwit

Nan istwa sa a, naratè a kòmanse pa fè lektè yo konnen li pa yon moun fou. Men, lektè yo dwe mande si li di laverite. Li kòmanse dekri ansasinay terib li fè sou yon nonm aje. L ap viv avèk nonm aje a, epi zye nonm aje a nui li. Naratè a konpare zye a ak zye yon votou. Paske zye a vin nuizib ofiramezi pou naratè a, li deside touye nonm aje a. Li vizite chanm nonm aje a pandan sèt (7) nwit swivi. Nan uityèm nwit lan, li touye li pandan son kè nonm aje a ap bat fò nan zòrèy li. Apre sa, li kache kò a anba planche a. Lapolis rive pou mennen ankèt. Naratè a kwè yo p ap jwenn anyen. Pita, pandan li menm ak lapolis ap pale, li kòmanse tande yon son ki toufe.

Trái tim Kể chuyện

Edgar Allan Poe

Bối cảnh: Một ngôi nhà tối, đêm khuya

Người kể chuyện trong câu chuyện này bắt đầu kể cho độc giả rằng ông không bị mất trí. Tuy nhiên các độc giả phải băn khoăn liệu ông ta có nói thật không.

Ông bắt đầu mô tả vụ án mạng của ông với một ông già. Ông sống với một ông già, và mắt ông già này làm ông khó chịu. Người kể chuyện so sánh con mắt này với con mắt kẻ tham lam. Vì con mắt này ngày càng trở nên khó chịu đối với người kể chuyện nên ông quyết định giết ông già. Ông đến phòng ngủ của ông già bảy đêm liền. Vào đêm thứ tám, ông giết ông già trong khi nghe tiếng tim ông già đập mạnh bên tai ông. Sau đó ông giấu xác ông già dưới sàn nhà. Cảnh sát đến điều tra. Người kể chuyện tin rằng họ sẽ không tìm thấy gì. Sau đó, khi ông và cảnh sát nói chuyện, ông bắt đầu nghe thấy tiếng nói bị nghẹt.

THE TELL–TALE HEART

Text Analysis

SUSPENSE

Writers often "hook" readers by creating a sense of excitement, tension, dread, or fear about what will happen next. This feeling is called **suspense.** Techniques used by Edgar Allan Poe to develop suspense include:

- describing a character's anxiety or fear
- relating vivid descriptions of dramatic sights and sounds
- repeating words, phrases, or characters' actions

Directions: In the chart, record the techniques for creating suspense used in each section, and then rank the sections from 1–4, with 1 being the most suspenseful.

Rank				
Lines	1–78	79–111	112–133	134–152
Techniques	1.	1.	1.	1.
	2.	2.	2.	2.

THE TELL—TALE HEART

Text Analysis

SUSPENSE

Los escritores con frecuencia "enganchan" a los lectores creando un sentimiento de emoción, tensión, temor o miedo sobre lo que va a pasar después. Este sentimiento se llama **suspenso.** Las técnicas usadas por Edgar Allan Poe para desarrollar suspenso incluyen:

- describir el temor o la ansiedad del personaje.
- relatar descripciones vívidas de vistas y sonidos dramáticos.
- palabras, frases o acciones repetidas de los personajes.

Instrucciones: En la gráfica, registra las técnicas para crear suspenso usadas en cada sección y después clasifica las secciones de 1–4, siendo 1 la de mayor suspenso.

Rango				
Líneas	1–78	79–111	112–133	134–152
Técnicas	1. 2.	1. 2.	1. 2.	1. 2.

THE TELL–TALE HEART
Reading Skill

EVALUATE NARRATOR

Have you ever suspected someone was not telling you the truth? Just as you can't trust every person you meet, you can't believe all **narrators,** or characters who tell a story. To evaluate a narrator's **reliability,** or trustworthiness, pay attention to his or her actions, attitudes, and statements. Do any raise your suspicions?

Directions: In the chart, record any clues that reveal whether the narrator is reliable or not.

Narrator's Reliability	
Makes Me Suspicious:	**Makes Me Trust Him:**
•	•
•	•
•	•
•	•
•	•

EL CORAZÓN DELATOR

Reading Skill

EVALUATE NARRATOR

¿Has sospechado alguna vez que alguien no te estaba diciendo la verdad? Así como no puedes confiar en todas las personas que conoces, no puedes creerle a todos los **narradores,** o personajes que cuentan un relato. Para evaluar la **confiabilidad** de un narrador, o su probidad, pon atención a sus acciones, actitudes y declaraciones. ¿Alguna de éstas aumentó tus sospechas?

Instrucciones: En la gráfica, anota cualquier indicio que revele si el narrador es o no confiable.

Confiabilidad del narrador	
Me hace sospechar de él:	**Me hace confiar en él:**
•	•
•	•
•	•
•	•
•	•

THE TELL–TALE HEART

Vocabulary Study

STORY PREDICTIONS

A. Directions: Listen as your teacher reads each sentence about "The Tell–Tale Heart." Together discuss what you know about the word or how it might be used. Write your ideas on the lines.

1. My hearing is **acute;** I can hear sounds that no one else notices.

   _____

2. My plan is daring; its **audacity** is unequaled.

   _____

3. I **conceived** a terrible thought.

   _____

4. A shaft of light appeared through the **crevice** in the door.

   _____

5. The others seemed to mock me; I could not stand their **derision.**

   _____

6. I knew what they were really thinking behind their **hypocritical** smiles.

   _____

7. **Stealthily,** I crept through the house.

   _____

8. He tried not to make a sound but let out a **stifled** groan.

   _____

9. I had no concern whatsoever that anyone would **vex** me.

   _____

10. As I argued my point, I spoke more loudly and **vehemently.**

    _____

THE TELL–TALE HEART

COPY MASTER

Vocabulary Practice

acute	derision	vehemently	crevice	stifled
conceive	stealthily	audacity	hypocritical	vex

A. Directions: Write the word from the box that correctly completes each sentence.

1. After Eli guessed the book's ending, he _____ denied having read ahead.

2. Most dogs don't see well, but they do have an _____ sense of smell.

3. The mountain climber's camera fell into a deep _____.

4. The boys crept _____ around the old haunted house.

5. Dom was the object of his team's _____ after striking out to end the game.

6. Gina thinks it _____ to chat with a friend and then talk behind her back.

7. Walter liked to _____ his grandfather by hiding his reading glasses.

8. Linda was proud that she could _____ the idea of writing an original play.

9. Being polite, John _____ a yawn during the lecture.

10. Eva was shocked that some people had the _____ to show up at her party without being invited.

B. Directions: For each word in the first column, find the word in the second column that is closest in meaning. Write the letter of that phrase in the blank.

____	**1.** acute	**a.**	smothered
____	**2.** vex	**b.**	ridicule
____	**3.** stifled	**c.**	annoy
____	**4.** derision	**d.**	boldness
____	**5.** audacity	**e.**	keen

THE TELL–TALE HEART

Vocabulary Strategy

USING REFERENCE AIDS

Choosing the perfect word can make a difference between good and great writing. One reason Poe's writing is still so popular is because of his masterful use of language. When you want to find the most accurate words to express yourself, the following reference aids can help you.

- A **thesaurus** is a reference book of **synonyms,** words with similar meanings. Most word processing programs provide an electronic thesaurus tool.
  afflictverb agonize, strike, torment, torture
- A **dictionary** lists synonyms after the definitions of some words.
  afflict (ə-flĭ' ĭkt´) v. To inflict grievous physical or mental suffering on.
  Syn: AGONIZE, TORMENT, TORTURE, RACK

Directions: Use a dictionary or thesaurus to find a synonym for each of the following words. Use each synonym in a sentence that utilizes its distinct meaning.

1. abandoned

_____

_____

2. paltry

_____

_____

3. inevitable

_____

_____

4. dissipated

_____

_____

5. credible

_____

_____

6. inevitable

_____

_____

THE TELL–TALE HEART   COPY MASTER

Reading Check

Directions: Recall all characters and events in the selection. Then answer each question in sentences or phrases.

1. Why do you think the narrator begins the story by telling us that he is not mad?

_____

_____

_____

2. Why did the narrator visit the old man's room seven nights in a row?

_____

_____

_____

3. Do you think the police could hear the heart beating? Why or why not?

_____

_____

_____

4. What do you really think caused the narrator to confess?

_____

_____

_____

5. Do you think the narrator was mad? Why or why not?

_____

_____

_____

THE TELL–TALE HEART

THE TELL–TALE HEART

Question Support

TEXT ANALYSIS

For questions 1–3, see page 88 of the Student Edition.

Directions: Answer the questions.

4. **Make Inferences** Reread lines 7–13. What can you infer about the relationship between the narrator and the old man?

   _____

   _____

   _____

5. **Analyze Suspense** Circle one of the phrases in parentheses and then complete the sentence.

   (Describing a character's anxiety or fear/Relating vivid descriptions of dramatic sights and sounds/Repeating words, phrases, or characters' actions) is the most effective technique that Poe used for creating suspense because _____

   _____

   _____

6. **Evaluate Narrator** Circle a choice in parentheses and then complete the sentence.

   The narrator in "The Tell-Tale Heart" is (reliable/not reliable) because _____

   _____

   _____

7. **Compare and Contrast** Circle a choice in parentheses and then complete the sentence.

   The narrator keeps saying that he is sane, but the reader knows that he is (wise/crazy). For the reader, this knowledge creates a feeling of tension, or suspense, because _____

   _____

   _____

THE TELL–TALE HEART   COPY MASTER

Reading Fluency

READING WITH EXPRESSION

When reading a horror story aloud, a dramatic reading can help create the proper mood. It can also help listeners visualize the setting and connect with the characters. Here are some tips to help you read with expression.

- Read at a natural pace, or speed. Try not to read word by word.
- Change the volume of your voice to emphasize key words or ideas.
- Vary the pitch of your voice, making it rise and fall, to avoid sounding dull. A change in pitch can add meaning to your words.
- Group words into meaningful phrases. Pause to signal the end of a thought or idea.

Directions: Follow along as your teacher reads this excerpt from "The Tell-Tale Heart." Notice where your teacher changes volume or pitch, stresses certain words, and pauses or stops. Then prepare your own reading of the passage, using these marks:

L = louder	↑ = raise pitch	/ = pause or stop
S = softer	↓ = lower pitch	underscore = add stress

True!—nervous—very, very dreadfully nervous I had been and am! but

why *will* you say that I am mad? The disease had sharpened my senses—not

destroyed—not dulled them. Above all was the sense of hearing acute.

I heard all things in the heaven and in the earth. I heard many things in hell.

How, then, am I mad? Hearken! and observe how healthily—how calmly

I can tell you the whole story.

    It is impossible to say how first the idea entered my brain; but once

conceived, it haunted me day and night. Object there was none. Passion

there was none. I loved the old man. He had never wronged me. He had

never given me insult. For his gold I had no desire. I think it was his

eye! Yes, it was this! He had the eye of a vulture—a pale blue eye with

a film over it. Whenever it fell upon me, my blood ran cold; and so by

degrees—very gradually—I made up my mind to take the life of the old

man and thus rid myself of the eye forever. (189 words)

                    —Edgar Allan Poe, from "The Tell-Tale Heart" Ideas for Extension

The Hitchhiker

Lucille Fletcher

WHY THIS SELECTION?

This radio play is a classic that belongs in every student's repertoire. Its suspenseful plot keeps readers on the edge of their seats as they try to figure out what will happen next.

ABOUT THIS SELECTION

Student/Teacher's Edition Pages: 90–103
Difficulty Level: Average

Summary Ronald Adams leaves his home in New York City to drive to California. While crossing the Brooklyn Bridge, he swerves to avoid hitting a hitchhiker. As he continues westward, he encounters this same man with increasing regularity. His sense of panic increases when he realizes that no one else can see the man. By the time Adams arrives in Gallup, New Mexico, he is beside himself with fear and uncertainty. He calls home. The woman who answers tells him that his mother is in the hospital, overcome with grief over the death of her son Ronald who was in a car accident on the Brooklyn Bridge six days before.

Engaging the Students This play offers students an opportunity to explore the key idea of proof. As Ronald Adams continues to see the mysterious presence of the hitchhiker, he becomes increasingly desperate to prove that the man exists. As students read the play, they are drawn into the character's dilemma and challenged to find proof one way or the other.

COMMON CORE STANDARDS FOCUS

- Foreshadowing
- Reading a Radio Play

LESSON RESOURCES

Plan and Teach

Student Copy Masters

ⓘ Lesson resources are also available on the **Teacher One Stop DVD-ROM** and online at **thinkcentral.com**.

Lesson Plan and Resource Guide

The Hitchhiker
Radio Play by Lucille Fletcher

Common Core Focus

RL 3 Analyze how particular lines of dialogue or incidents in a story propel the action, reveal aspects of a character, or provoke a decision. **RL 5** Compare and contrast the structure of two or more texts. **W 1** Write arguments to support claims with clear reasons and relevant evidence. **L 1** Demonstrate command of standard English grammar when writing.

Unless otherwise noted, all resources can be found in the *Resource Manager*.
ℹ️ Lesson resources are also available on the **Teacher One Stop DVD-ROM** and online at **thinkcentral.com.** The Student Edition and selected copy masters are available electronically on the �’ **Student One Stop DVD-ROM.**

Student/Teacher's Edition Pages	Additional Resources CM = Copy Master T = Transparency
Focus and Motivate	
❏ Big Question p. 90	
❏ Author Biography and Background Information p. 91	❏ ℹ️ Literature and Reading Center at **thinkcentral.com**
Teach	
❏ Foreshadowing p. 91	❏ Foreshadowing CM— English p. 105, Spanish p. 106 🄳
❏ Reading a Radio Play p. 91	
❏ Vocabulary in Context p. 91	❏ Vocabulary Study CM p. 109 🄳

🄳 = Resources for Differentiation

Student/Teacher's Edition Pages	Additional Resources CM = Copy Master T = Transparency

Practice and Apply: Guided Practice

Selection and Teacher Notes	❑ ✐ **Audio Anthology CD** D
❑ *The Hitchhiker,* pp. 92–101	❑ Summary CM—English and Spanish p. 103, Haitian Creole and Vietnamese p. 104 D
	❑ Reading Fluency CM p. 113
	❑ 🧰 **Best Practices Toolkit**
	❑ Sequence Chain p. B21, B45 [T] D
	❑ Cause-and-Effect Diagram pp. B16, B38 [T] D
	❑ ℹ Audio Summaries at **thinkcentral.com**

Practice and Apply: After Reading

❑ Selection Questions p. 102	❑ Reading Check CM p. 110
	❑ Reading a Radio Play CM—p. 107, Spanish p. 108 D
	❑ Question Support CM p. 111 D
	❑ Additional Selection Questions p. 99 D
	❑ Ideas for Extension p. 100 D
❑ Grammar in Context p. 103 ❑ Writing Prompt p. 103	❑ Maintain Pronoun-Antecedent Agreement CM p. 112
	❑ Grammar Handbook—Student Edition p. R52
	❑ ℹ GrammarNotes DVD-ROM at **thinkcentral.com**
	❑ ℹ Interactive Revision Lessons on WriteSmart CD-ROM and online at **thinkcentral.com**

D = Resources for Differentiation

THE HITCHHIKER

Student/Teacher's Edition Pages	Additional Resources CM = Copy Master T = Transparency
Assess and Reteach	
Assess	❑ **Diagnostic and Selection Tests** ❑ Selection Tests A, B/C pp. 39–40, 41–42 Ⓓ ❑ ⓘ ThinkCentral Online Assessment ❑ ✏ ExamView Test Generator on the **Teacher One Stop DVD-ROM**
Reteach ❑ Foreshadowing ❑ Reading a Radio Play ❑ Pronoun-Antecedent Agreement	❑ ⓘ Level Up Online Tutorials on **thinkcentral.com** ❑ ⓘ Reteaching Worksheets on **thinkcentral.com** ❑ Literature Lesson 8: Foreshadowing and Suspense ❑ Literature Lesson 25: Elements of Drama ❑ Grammar Lesson 10: Antecedent Agreement with Indefinite Pronouns

Ⓓ = Resources for Differentiation

Additional Selection Questions

Use to supplement the questions on SE page 102.

Differentiation Use these questions to provide customized practice with comprehension and critical thinking skills.

Easy

1. **Is seeing BELIEVING?**
Is there any proof that the hitchhiker exists? (*No. No other character can see him, including the mechanic and the girl that Adams picks up. Also he is seen in the most improbable places toward the end of the play.*)

2. **Identify Foreshadowing** What might Mrs. Adams's comment at the beginning of the play foreshadow? Explain. (*Since Mrs. Adams is so careful to warn her son, her comment might foreshadow something bad happening, even though he reassures her that he willbe fine.*)

3. **Recall** When does Adams start to think that there is something odd about his sighting of the hitchhiker? (*After Adams sees the hitchhiker the third time on the first day of his journey, he begins to get nervous. That is when he stops at the gas station.*)

Average

4. **Is seeing BELIEVING?**
What proves to the roadside stand owner that Adams is a suspicious character? (*He comes in the middle of the night. He won't leave. He talks about someone the owner didn't see.*)

5. **Analyze Foreshadowing** In what ways is the more frequent appearance of the hitchhiker as the play goes on an example of foreshadowing? (*The hitchhiker's almost constant presence suggests that Adams cannot escape his fate.*)

6. **Reading a Radio Play** What function does the music in this play serve? (*The music indicates scene changes and builds mood.*)

Challenging

7. **Is seeing BELIEVING?**
Is the phone call home definite proof that Adams is dead? Why or why not? (*Yes. Mrs. Whitney says that he is. No. He might be just imagining the phone call. It could be a manifestation of his confused mental state.*)

8. **Evaluate Foreshadowing** In lines 80–81, Adams says that he is looking forward to the drive, even to the loneliness. In what way is this example of foreshadowing also ironic? (*It may be his solitude that leads to his delusion that the hitchhiker is pursuing him. Also, later in the play, in lines 311–315, Adams decides that he cannot stand to be alone. He wants someone with him constantly.*)

THE HITCHHIKER

Ideas for Extension

Differentiation These activities provide students with a variety of options for demonstrating understanding of lesson concepts.

EXPLORATIONS AND ACTIVITIES

MAP ROUTE: EXPLORE SETTING

Point out that several specific locations, such as Hollywood and the Brooklyn Bridge, are mentioned in the play.

Divide the class into small groups. Have students use the information about the places Adams passes through and the roads he takes to create a road map of the route that someone might travel to get from New York City to Hollywood. Students can use an atlas to estimate the number of miles he would cover and how long the journey might take him, including time built in for stops.

Compare routes and talk about what a modern-day traveler could expect to find on these roads in contrast to Adams's experience. What kinds of different environments would a traveler on those routes pass through? In what ways might those environments add to the atmosphere of the play?

MUSIC SELECTION: CONVEY MOOD

Remind students that the music is an important element of this radio play. As a class, list all the lines in which a reference to music appears.

Divide the lines up and then have small groups of students work together to choose musical selections that they think would fit the plot and mood of the play at each point. Tell students that they need only a few bars in most cases and they might want to use the same piece more than once.

Have students perform the relevant parts of the play, incorporating their chosen music. Hold a class vote on the effectiveness of each group's choices. Discuss how hearing the music adds to the feeling conveyed by the dialogue.

POSTER: INTERPRET CHARACTER AND PLOT

Have students imagine that *The Hitchhiker* is going to be presented on the school radio station and they are in charge of publicity.

Working in groups or alone, students should create a poster advertising the upcoming show. Remind students that their posters need to excite interest in the program and represent what it is about without giving away the plot. Encourage students to incorporate text and graphics into their posters and to use colors that effectively convey the mood that they want the potential audience to feel.

Ask students to display their posters and compare the elements of each.

CONFLICT CHART: ANALYZE PLOT

Throughout the play, Adams experiences both internal and external conflicts.

Ask small groups to trace and identify each conflict in a chart. Have them describe it and explain whether it is resolved or unresolved at the end of the play.

Groups may then wish to compare their charts and use the information to create a map of the story's conflicts.

COMPARISON: EXAMINE CHARACTER

Discuss how much Adams changes throughout the play. Have students reread lines 47–82 and then 371–489 to help illustrate the difference in his state of mind.

Ask students to compare and contrast Adams at the start of his journey and at the end. Students should focus on details that are stated and should also make inferences about his character. For example, he appears to be going to Hollywood for a reason, suggesting that he is gainfully employed and therefore a responsible person. His mother shows no fears about his mental state, nor does he when he first sets off.

Ask students to organize their comparisons in a Venn diagram.

INQUIRY AND RESEARCH

GAS PRICES

At one point in the play, Adams pays one dollar and forty-nine cents to fill up his car after traveling most of the day. Obviously in the 21st century, gas expenses would take a much greater part of his budget.

Assign groups of students one of these time periods: 1940s, 1950s, 1960s, 1970s, 1980s, 1990s, and 2000 through the present year. Ask groups to track the gas prices for their era. Students should collect their data in a table. They might find their information on the Internet or ask a librarian for assistance with print resources.

Have groups present their tables to the class. Then have the class collaborate on a line graph that shows the changes in gas prices from the 1940s to today. As a class, draw conclusions from the data, such as when gas prices were most stable and during which time period the cost rose the most.

Pre-AP Challenge: In addition to tracing the increase in gas costs, have groups of students at the same time find information on the changes in the average income over their decade. Students should identify the income at the beginning and end of their decade. After students have presented both sets of data to the class, have them draw a line graph with two lines, showing the increase of both gas costs and income over the past several decades. Encourage students to draw some conclusions from their graph about the relationship between the two sets of data.

WRITING

EVALUATE ELEMENTS OF DRAMA: REVIEW

Ask students to write a review of the play for their local newspaper, in which they analyze the strengths and weaknesses that they perceive in it. Remind students that for each opinion they state, they should offer support in the form of details from the text. Students' reviews should also convey clearly whether or not they recommend the play.

Teacher Notes

Review and Evaluate Outcome
What did I want students to know or be able to do?
How successful was the lesson?

Evaluate Process
What worked? • Strategies   • Resources   • Differentiation   What did not work? Why not?

Reflect
The next time I teach "The Hitchhiker," what will I do differently? Why?

Plan Ahead
What must I do next?

THE HITCHHIKER
Summary

THE HITCHHIKER
Lucille Fletcher
Setting: Various locations across the United States; 1940s

Ronald Adams is driving from New York to Hollywood, California. Before he leaves on the trip, his mother warns him to be careful along the way, not to pick up hitchhikers or drive too fast. As he crosses the Brooklyn Bridge, a hitchhiker steps off the pavement in front of him. Adams has to swerve to avoid hitting him. He sees the same hitchhiker a few times along his route, and then more and more frequently. He thinks the man may be trying to harm him or even kill him. By the time Adams arrives in Gallup, New Mexico, he wonders if he is going crazy. No hitchhiker could keep up with someone driving a car, and yet Adams continues to see the same man. Finally, he calls his mother. He thinks the sound of her voice will make him feel better, however, a strange woman answers his mother's phone.

EL VAGABUNDO
Lucille Fletcher
Escenario: Varias localidades a lo largo de Los Estados Unidos, los años cuarenta

Ronald Adams va a conducir desde Nueva York hasta Hollywood. Antes de iniciar su viaje, su madre lo previene de tener cuidado a lo largo del camino, de no subir vagabundos o de no conducir muy rápido. Mientras cruza el Puente de Brooklyn, un vagabundo se le cruza. Adams tiene que hacerse a un lado para evitar golpearlo. él ve al mismo vagabundo algunas veces a lo largo del camino, y después cada vez con mayor frecuencia. Piensa que el hombre tal vez esté intentando lastimarlo o hasta matarlo. Para cuando Adams llega a Gallup, Nuevo México, se empieza a preguntar si se estará volviendo loco. Ningún vagabundo podría seguirle el paso a alguien conduciendo un auto y, aún así Adams continúa viendo al mismo hombre. Finalmente, le llama a su madre. él piensa que el sonido de su voz lo va a hacer sentirse mejor, sin embargo, una mujer extraña contesta el teléfono de su madre.

THE HITCHHIKER
Summary

MOUN K AP RETE MACHIN
Lucille Fletcher

Espas ak tan: Divès kote nan Etazini; ane 1940 yo

Wonal Adams ap kondi ant Nouyòk ak Aliwoud, Kalifòni. Anvan li koumanse vwayaj la, manman li avèti li pou li pridan sou tout wout la, pou li pa pran moun k ap rete machin nan lari oswa pou li pa kondi vit. Pandan li travèse Pon Bwouklin nan, yon moun parèt nan mitan lari a devan li. Adams dwe devye pou li pa frape li. Li wè menm moun plizyè fwa toutolon wout la, epi plizanpli li wè li pi souvan. Li panse nonm lan ka ap eseye fè li mal oswa menm touye li. Nan moman Adams rive nan Galòp, Nyou Meksiko, li mande si se pa fou l ap vin fou. Okenn moun k ap rete machin pa ka swiv yon moun k ap kondi yon oto, epoutan Adams kontinye wè menm nonm lan. Finalman, li rele manman li. Li panse son vwa manman li ap fè li santi li pi byen, men, yon fi etranj reponn nan telefòn manman li.

Người vẫy xe đi nhờ
Lucille Fletcher

Bối cảnh: Nhiều địa điểm khác nhau trên khắp nước Mỹ; những năm 1940

Ronald Adams lái xe từ New York đến Hollywood, California. Trước khi anh chuẩn bị cho một chuyến đi, mẹ anh cảnh báo anh phải cẩn thận dọc đường, không đón những người vẫy xe đi nhờ hoặc lái xe quá nhanh. Khi anh đi qua Brooklyn Bridge, một vẫy xe đi nhờ bước tới mặt đường trước mặt anh. Adams phải quẹo đi để tránh đâm phải ông ta. Anh cũng nhìn thấy chính người vẫy xe này vài lần trên tuyến đường của anh, và sau đó mỗi lúc anh lại càng nhìn thấy người đó nhiều lần hơn lên. Anh nghĩ rằng người đàn ông này có thể đang định làm hại anh hoặc thậm chí là giết anh. Khi Adams đến Gallup, New Mexico, anh băn khoăn liệu anh có bị điên không. Không có người vẫy xe dọc đường nào có thể đuổi kịp một người đang lái xe, và Adams lại tiếp tục nhìn thấy người đàn ông đó. Cuối cùng anh gọi điện cho mẹ anh. Anh nghĩ rằng tiếng của mẹ anh sẽ làm anh cảm thấy dễ chịu hơn, tuy nhiên, người đàn ông lạ mặt trả lời bằng điện thoại của mẹ anh.

THE HITCHHIKER

Text Analysis

FORESHADOWING

While reading a story or watching a movie, have you ever gotten a hint about what might happen later on? A device that prepares readers for an event or action occurring later in the plot is called **foreshadowing.** Anticipating the next event can make you more excited to find out about what happens next.

Directions: In the chart, record events or dialogue that might foreshadow what happens later.

Foreshadowing	Events That Were Foreshadowed

THE HITCHHIKER

EL VAGABUNDO

Text Analysis

FORESHADOWING

Mientras lees un relato o miras una película, ¿has alguna vez predicho lo que va a suceder más tarde? El dispositivo que prepara a los lectores para un acontecimiento o acción que ocurrirá más adelante en la trama se le llama **presagio.** Anticipar el siguiente acontecimiento puede motivarte a saber qué va a suceder después.

Instrucciones: En la gráfica, anota acontecimientos o el diálogo que pueda presagiar lo que sucederá después.

Presagio	Acontecimientos que fueron presagiados

SPANISH

THE HITCHHIKER

Reading Strategy

READING A RADIO PLAY

A **radio play** is a play written for radio broadcast, which means that it was originally meant to be heard, not seen. When you're reading a radio play, you'll understand it best if you try to imagine what it would sound like being performed. As you read, look for the following elements:

- **Stage directions** or instructions, for the actor will help you know how a line is spoken.
- **Sound effects** are often used to suggest what is happening in the play. They help a listener "see" the action.
- the term music will indicate when and sometimes what kind of music is used to mark a change of scene or show the passing of time.

Directions: Reread lines 381–419. Then complete the following sentence.

Without the sound effects and stage directions, I would not know

_____

_____

_____

_____

_____

_____

_____

_____

_____

_____

_____

_____

_____

THE HITCHHIKER

EL VAGABUNDO

Reading Strategy

READING A RADIO PLAY

Una **comedia radiofónica** es una comedia escrita para transmitirse por la radio, lo que significa que fue hecha con la intención original de escucharse, no de ser vista. Cuando lees una comedia radiofónica, la puedes entender mejor si tratas de imaginar cómo sonaría si se representara. Mientras lees, busca los siguientes elementos.

- Las **direcciones de escena,** o instrucciones para el actor, te ayudarán a saber cómo se dice una línea.
- Los **efectos de sonido** con frecuencia se usan para sugerir lo que está sucediendo en la comedia. Ayudan al oyente a "ver" la acción.
- El término *música* indicará cuándo y, algunas veces, qué tipo de música se usa para marcar el cambio de escena o mostrar el paso del tiempo.

Instruccioness: Vuelve a leer las líneas 381-419. Después completa la siguiente oración.

Sin los efectos de sonido y sin las direcciones de escena no sabría

_____

_____

_____

_____

_____

_____

_____

_____

_____

_____

_____

_____

SPANISH

COPY MASTER

Vocabulary Study

VOCABULARY IN CONTEXT

A. Directions: As your teacher reads each set of sentences, listen for the boldfaced word and clues to its possible meaning.

1. Adams gave his mother his solemn **assurance** that he would drive safely.

2. He thought the journey across country would be a **lark;** he was looking forward to it.

3. The **monotony** of miles and miles of flat highway was interrupted by the sight of the hitchhiker at the side of the road.

4. Although there was nothing **sinister** or threatening about the hitchhiker's appearance, seeing him filled Adams with fear.

5. When Adams noticed the hitchhiker at the railroad **junction,** he immediately drove across the tracks toward him.

B. Directions: To determine how well you understand each vocabulary word, fill in the chart. As you read the selection, revise your definitions as needed.

Vocabulary Word	New	Seen Before	Can Use in a Sentence	Possible Meanings
1. assurance				
2. lark				
3. monotony				
4. sinister				
5. junction				

THE HITCHHIKER

Reading Check

Directions: Recall all characters and events in the selection. Then answer each question in sentences or phrases.

1. What inference would you make about the relationship between Adams and his mother?

   _____

   _____

   _____

2. What is Ronald Adam's mood as he says goodbye to his mother and sets off on his journey?

   _____

   _____

   _____

3. How does Ronald Adams describe the hitchhiker's appearance?

   _____

   _____

   _____

4. Why does the girl jump out of Ronald Adams's car?

   _____

   _____

   _____

5. By the time Ronald Adams is driving the road between Albuquerque and Gallup, where is he seeing the hitchhiker?

   _____

   _____

   _____

THE HITCHHIKER

Question Support

TEXT ANALYSIS

For questions 1–3, see page 102 of the Student Edition.

Directions: Answer the questions.

4. **Make Inferences** Reread lines 49–77. Describe the relationship between Adams and his mother.

_____

_____

5. **Examine Foreshadowing Foreshadowing** prepares readers for an event or action that occurs later in the plot. Complete the sentence.

In this radio play, the most effective use of foreshadowing in creating suspense is _____

_____

_____

6. **Analyze the Radio Play** If sound effects and stage directions were taken out of the play, do you think listeners would fully understand what was happening? Explain your answer.

_____

_____

_____

7. **Draw Conclusions** Complete the sentence.

In the radio play, the hitchhiker is _____

_____

8. **Compare Across Texts** Name one similarity and one difference that you found in "The Tell-Tale Heart" and *The Hitchhiker*.

_____

_____

_____

_____

_____

THE HITCHHIKER

THE HITCHHIKER

Grammar in Context

MAINTAIN PRONOUN-ANTECEDENT AGREEMENT

An **antecedent** is the noun or pronoun to which a pronoun refers. In the following
sentence, the plural pronoun *their* refers to the antecedent *they: They took their seats
at the café.* Use singular pronouns with singular antecedents and plural pronouns
with plural antecedents. Pair antecedents ending in *one, thing,* or *body* with singular
pronouns, such as he, her, she, or his.

> *Original:* Adams would ask just about **anyone** whether **they** had seen the
> hitchhiker.

> *Revised:* Adams would ask just about **anyone** whether **he or she** had seen the
> hitchhiker.

Directions: Rewrite each sentence, correcting the pronoun-antecedent error or
errors.

1. No one in their right mind woud want to get a ride from Adams.

   _____

   _____

2. Everybody knows that they shouldn't pick up hitchhikers.

   _____

   _____

3. Anyone with common sense should realize that they would be putting
   themselves in danger.

   _____

   _____

4. Nobody could convince me that they had seen this man on the side of the road.

   _____

   _____

5. If anyone ever told me that this experience happened to them, I wouldn't believe it.

   _____

   _____

THE HITCHHIKER

Reading Fluency

READERS THEATER

Readers Theater is a way of performing a play in which the actors read their parts from a script. Using only their voices, the actors make the characters come alive for the audience. They may also add to the atmosphere by using their voices to create sound effects. You can perform most plays as Readers Theater. To give a successful performance, follow these suggestions:

- Read at a natural pace, or speed, as you do when you talk. Adjust your pace to bring out the personality of your character.
- Experiment with phrasing. How you group words can sometime affect their meaning.
- Vary your pitch, making your voice rise and fall, to express emotion and to keep listeners interested.
- Speak louder or softer to call attention to important words or ideas.
- Imitate the sound effects as realistically as possible.

A. Directions: With a partner, perform lines 80-119 of *The Hitchhiker* as Readers Theater. One person should read Adam's lines. The other will provide the sound effects and perform the part of Voice. Fill in the chart to explain how to read your character's lines or how to make the sound effects.

Character:
Description:
Manner of Speaking:
Speaking Rate:

B. Directions: Now perform the scene for your class. Evaluate your performance on the lines below.

_____

_____

_____

_____

HOOT

Text Analysis

IDENTIFY GENRE FEATURES

What makes a book a **mystery novel**? First you need a crime or explained event. Look for clues left behind and motives for what happened. Suspense will build as further clues are revealed. There may even be a plot twist or two.

Directions: In the chart, record an example of each element of a mystery novel. One example has been done for you.

Characteristics of a Mystery Novel	Example
Crime or Unexplained Event	Roy sees a "weird" kid at one of the bus stops.
Clues and/or Motives	
Suspense	
Plot Twist	

HOOT

Media Study | The Sisterhood of the Traveling Pants

WHAT'S THE CONNECTION?

This Media Study reinforces the unit focus on plot and conflict. Filmmakers create plot by introducing characters, their relationships, and their problems and getting viewers to care about these characters. Students will learn how filmmakers use elements such as blocking, close-up and medium shots, and music to develop plot and conflict. Students will also examine the ways in which filmmakers get viewers emotionally involved in stories.

ABOUT THE MEDIA STUDY

Student/Teacher's Edition Pages: 110–113

Summary In this clip from the feature film *The Sisterhood of the Traveling Pants,* teenager Carmen has just traveled to spend the summer with her father. She looks forward to spending quality time alone with him. However, from the time he picks her up at the train station until their arrival at his home, she is dealt one surprise after another—he has moved, he is living with someone who has teenage children, and he is getting married at the end of the summer.

Engaging the Students Throughout the Media Study, students explore the key concept of how filmmakers use specific techniques to create memorable movie versions of books.

LESSON RESOURCES
Plan and Teach

Student Copy Masters

ⓘ Lesson resources are also available on the **Teacher One Stop DVD-ROM** and online at **thinkcentral.com**.

MEDIA STUDY: *from THE* SISTERHOOD . . . .

Lesson Plan and Resource Guide

Media Study: *from* The Sisterhood of the Traveling Pants
Film Clip

Common Core Focus

RL 7 Analyze a filmed production, evaluating the choices made by the director.

Unless otherwise noted, all resources can be found in the *Resource Manager*.
ⓘ Lesson resources are also available on the **Teacher One Stop DVD-ROM** and online at **thinkcentral.com.** The Student Edition and selected copy masters are available electronically on the ⬭ **Student One Stop DVD-ROM.**

Student/Teacher's Edition Pages	Additional Resources CM = Copy Master T = Transparency
Focus and Motivate	
❑ Big Question p. 110	❑ Summary CM—English and Spanish, p. 119, Haitian Creole and Vietnamese p. 120 ⒹＤ
Teach	
❑ Media Literacy: Plot in Movies p. 111	❑ ⬭ **Media*Smart* DVD-ROM** ❑ Introduction, First Viewing, Media Lessons
Practice and Apply: Guided Practice	
❑ Viewing Guide and Teacher Notes p. 112	❑ Viewing Guide CM p. 121 ❑ Close Viewing CM p. 122 ❑ Media Activity CM p. 123 ❑ ⬭ **Media*Smart* DVD-ROM** ❑ Guided Analysis ❑ Ideas for Extension p.117
Assess and Reteach	
Assess ❑ Write or Discuss p. 113 ❑ Produce Your Own Media p. 113	❑ Produce Your Own Media CM p. 124 ❑ ⬭ **Media*Smart* DVD-ROM** ❑ ⓘ **MediaScope** at **thinkcentral.com**
Reteach ❑ Plot in Movies	

Ⓓ = Resources for Differentiation

Ideas for Extension

Differentiation These activities provide students with a variety of options for demonstrating understanding of lesson concepts.

EXPLORATIONS AND ACTIVITIES

SOUNDTRACK: EXAMINE DIALOGUE AND MUSIC

Remind students that directors use sound elements such as dialogue and background music to stir the emotions of viewers and encourage them to care about characters. Divide the class into pairs or small groups. Have students choose a scene from a story or play that includes dialogue between characters. Students should discuss, in their groups or with their partner, how they feel about the characters who are speaking and what they learn about them through their dialogue. Then have students select background music that would be appropriate for the mood of the scene.

Have students rehearse and present the scene to the rest of the class, reading the dialogue aloud, playing their musical selection in the background.

Pre-AP Challenge: Remind students that choices related to blocking, camera position, and sound can change the mood and the meaning expressed in a movie scene. Ask pairs to select a brief scene from a story or play. Ask them to plan two versions of the scene, experimenting with the arrangement of characters within a film frame, use of close-up and medium shots, and use of music and sound.

INQUIRY AND RESEARCH

THE DIRECTOR'S CRAFT

Explain to students that the film industry has been represented by many well-known directors—each with his or her own style of telling stories. Have students select a film director to research. Their research should focus on specific films their director has created and the particular style he or she has in developing plot and engaging viewers. If students need help launching their research, you might tell them to identify the directors of some of their favorite films. If necessary, display a list of well-known directors and have them select one to research. Possible names include Frank Capra, Steven Spielberg, Ron Howard, Penny Marshall, and George Lucas.

Students should use their research to write a brief essay about their director. If possible, they should include a visual aid to help readers understand the director's style. This might be a drawing or an actual frame from a film that is available online.

WRITING

ANALYZE TECHNIQUES: MOVIE REVIEW

Invite students to review the video clip they have just seen, paying close attention to how well its director uses blocking, camera positioning, and other techniques to develop plot and encourage viewers to care about characters. Have students write a review in which they explain why the director was successful or unsuccessful in telling a story on the big screen. As students discuss the director's techniques, encourage them to use terminology presented in the Media Study (*exposition, character, setting, conflict, blocking, close-up shot,* and *medium shot*).

Teacher Notes

Review and Evaluate Outcome

What did I want students to know or be able to do?

Which Teaching Option did I use?

_____ Teaching Option 1: The Basics (1–2 days)

_____ Teaching Option 2: In-Depth Study (2–3 days)

How successful was the lesson?

Evaluate Process

What worked?

• Strategies

• Resources

What did not work? Why not?

Reflect

The next time I teach this Media Study, what will I do differently? Why?

Plan Ahead

What must I do next?

Summary

FROM THE SISTERHOOD OF THE TRAVELING PANTS

Bridget, Tibby, Lena, and Carmen have been best friends their entire lives. Just before they spend their first summer apart, the girls discover a pair of jeans that, amazingly, fits each of them. They decide to stay connected by sharing the jeans.

In this clip from the film adaptation of the novel, Carmen arrives in South Carolina to spend her summer vacation with her dad. Carmen is excited because she hasn't seen her father more than twice a year since her parents divorced. On the drive back from the train station, Carmen's dad reveals that he has a surprise but she's too caught up sharing her vacation plans. Before Carmen can ask what it is, she spots a woman who she thinks is a neighbor. Carmen learns that this woman is her father's new fiancée and that her father will marry her in just two months. Pay attention to how the positioning of the characters and the camera help draw you into the conflict.

TOMADO DE LA HERMANDAD DE LOS PANTALONES VIAJEROS

Bridget, Tibby, Lena, y Carmen han sido muy buenas amigas durante toda su vida. Justo antes de que ellas pasen su primer verano separadas, las chicas descubren un par de pantalones vaqueros que, sorprendentemente les quedan a todas. Deciden mantenerse en contacto compartiendo los pantalones vaqueros.

En esta selección de la adaptación fílmica de la novela, Carmen llega a Carolina del Sur para pasar sus vacaciones de verano con su papá. Carmen está muy emocionada porque no ha visto a su papá más de dos veces al año desde que sus padres se divorciaron. En el viaje de regreso desde la estación de tren, el papá de Carmen le revela que tiene una sorpresa, pero ella está muy ocupada compartiendo sus planes de vacaciones. Antes de que Carmen pueda preguntar qué es, ella ve a una mujer que cree que es la vecina. Carmen se entera de que esta mujer es la nueva prometida de su padre y de que se casarán en de dos meses. Pon atención a cómo la situación de los personajes y de la cámara ayudan a involucrarte en el conflicto.

Summary

FROM SOLIDARITE FANM POU PANTALON VWAYAJ

Bridjèt, Tiby, Lena, ak Kamèn se te bon zanmi pandan tout lavi yo. Anvan yo pase premye lete yo apa, medam yo dekouvri yon pantalon djin ki, pa chans, bon pou yo tout. Yo deside rete konekte nan mete pantalon djin nan.

Nan ekstrè fim sa a ki se adaptasyon woman an, Kamèn rive nan Kawolin-di-Sid pou l pase vakans lete li avèk papa li. Kamèn kontan anpil paske li pa wè paran li yo plis pase de (2) fwa chak ane depi paran l yo te divòse a. Lè l ap retounen sòti nan estasyon tren an, papa Kamèn fè li konnen li gen yon sipriz men manmzèl te twò prese pou li fè li konnen plan vakans li. Anvan pou Kamèn te ka mande sa li ye, li remake yon fi, li panse ki se yon vwazin. Kamèn vin konnen fi sa a se nouvo fiyanse papa li epi papa li pral marye ak li nan sèlman de (2) mwa. Fè atansyon ak fason pozisyon pèsonaj yo ak kamera a ede w antre nan konfli a.

trich từ TÌNH CHỊ EM CỦA CHIẾC QUẦN DU LỊCH

Bridget, Tibby, Lena, và Carmen là những người bạn thân nhất của nhau cả cuộc đời họ. Chỉ trước khi họ có kỳ nghỉ hè riêng đầu tiên của mình, những cô gái này tìm thấy một chiếc quần jean vừa cho tất cả các cô đến bất ngờ. Họ quyết định tiếp tục kết nghĩa với nhau bằng cách chung nhau chiếc quần jean này.

Trong đoạn phim chuyển thể từ tiểu thuyết này, Carmen đến Nam Carolina để nghỉ hè với cha cô. Carmen bị kích động vì cô chưa được gặp cha nhiều hơn hai lần mỗi năm từ khi cha mẹ cô ly dị. Trong khi lái xe từ bến tàu trở về, cha của Carmen tiết lộ rằng ông có một bất ngờ nhưng cô cũng bị ngắt lời khi đang chia sẻ các kế hoạch kỳ nghỉ của mình. Trước khi Carmen có thể hỏi đó là cái gì, cô nhận ra một phụ nữ mà cô nghĩ là một người hàng xóm. Carmen được biết rằng người phụ nữ này là vợ mới chưa cưới của cha cô và cha cô sẽ cưới bà trong hai tháng tới. Hãy chú ý vào cách đặt tình huống của các nhân vật và máy quay phim giúp dẫn dắt bạn vào mâu thuẫn đó.

MEDIA STUDY: *from* THE SISTERHOOD OF THE TRAVELING PANTS

COPY MASTER

Media Literacy: Plot in Movies

VIEWING GUIDE

The **exposition** stage of a movie is the part that introduces the characters, setting, and conflict. The first steps in developing a plot are to show the characters' relationships and struggles, and to help viewers understand and relate to them.

Directions: The first column of the chart lists the different storytelling techniques directors use. An example of each technique has been provided for you in the second column of the chart. As you view the clip, find a different example for each technique and describe it in the third column of the chart.

Storytelling Techniques	Example	What I Understand at This Point
Composition • *the arrangement of the characters within a film frame* *Effect: Portrays relationships between characters*	When you first see Carmen's dad, he is in the center of the shot.	
Camera Placement • *Close-up shot (a detailed view of a character or an object)* • *Medium shot (shows a character from the waist up)* *Effect: Reveals how characters are affected by what's happening*	A close-up shot of Carmen when her dad reveals his surprise.	
Music *Effect: Used to reflect a character's emotions*	The music you hear when Carmen arrives for her visit.	

MEDIA STUDY: *from* THE SISTERHOOD . . . .

MEDIA STUDY: *from* THE SISTERHOOD OF THE TRAVELING PANTS   COPY MASTER

Media Literacy: Plot in Movies

CLOSE VIEWING

Directors use different camera shots to help reveal how the characters are affected by what is happening onscreen. A **close-up shot** shows a detailed view of a character or object. Close-ups can also show a character's personality or emotions. A **medium shot** shows a character from the waist up, allowing the audience to see movements that reveal a character's behavior.

Directions: As you watch the clip, examine how the filmmakers use camera shots to hint at the developing conflict between Carmen and her father. Three different shots are listed in the first column of the chart. In the second column, describe the different emotions or reactions conveyed in the shot. Then, write down how this helps set up the conflict.

Camera shot	What kind of emotions or reactions are revealed in the shot?	How does this help develop conflict?
Medium shot of Carmen sitting in her father's car, opening a envelope.		
Close-up shot of Carmen as her dad drives up to the house and a woman comes out to greet them.		
Medium shot of Carmen standing next to the car by herself, as her father reveals his engagement.		

MEDIA STUDY: *from* THE SISTERHOOD . . .

MEDIA STUDY: *from* THE SISTERHOOD OF THE TRAVELING PANTS   COPY MASTER

Media Literacy: Plot in Movies

MEDIA ACTIVITY

The director of *The Sisterhood of the Traveling Pants* uses **blocking,** the arrangement of characters within a frame, and camera shots to portray characters and conflict. You can use these techniques to evaluate characters and conflict in other movies.

Directions: Think of a tense scene from another movie you have seen recently. Write its title on the line, and use the space provided to make a rough sketch of a shot from that scene. Then, answer the following questions to explain how the blocking and camera shots helped convey the conflict.

Title: _____

1. What does the composition of the shot reveal about the characters?

   _____

   _____

2. How do the camera shots help you understand the characters' emotions or reactions?

   _____

   _____

MEDIA STUDY: *from* THE SISTERHOOD . . . .

MEDIA STUDY: *from* THE SISTERHOOD OF THE TRAVELING PANTS   COPY MASTER

Media Literacy: **Plot in Movies**

PRODUCE YOUR OWN MEDIA

Directors use **storyboards** to plan how to shoot scenes in a film. Each frame of the storyboard is made up of a sketch and a short description of what will be happening onscreen. The descriptions tell what kind of camera shots will be used, what action will be taking place, and what sounds will be heard during a specific scene.

Directions: Choose an important scene from a novel you've read recently or one of the stories from this unit. With a partner, create a storyboard that shows a conflict from your story. Use the boxes to make a simple sketch of each shot and describe what the viewer will see and hear onscreen. Use the back of this sheet, if necessary.

Shot type:
Action:
Audio:

Shot type:
Action:
Audio:

Shot type:
Action:
Audio:

Shot type:
Action:
Audio:

MEDIA STUDY: *from* THE SISTERHOOD . . .

Lesson at a Glance

My First Free Summer

JULIA ALVAREZ

WHY THIS SELECTION?

Julia Alvarez is an extremely popular author of fiction, poetry, and nonfiction—including several books for young readers. This memoir will interest students, motivating them to understand how political events have an impact on their lives.

ABOUT THIS SELECTION

Student/Teacher's Edition Pages: 114–121
Difficulty Level: Easy
Readability Scores: Lexile: 820; Fry: 7; Dale-Chall: 6.3

Summary Tired of attending summer school, Alvarez works hard in fifth grade and finally gets her "first free summer." She is unable to enjoy it, however, as the political situation in her homeland, the Dominican Republic, is rapidly deteriorating. The safety of Alvarez's family is threatened, and they flee to the United States.

Engaging the Students Like Alvarez, most students will have had the experience of leaving a person or place that has helped them feel safe and secure. As students read the memoir, they have the opportunity to reflect on how this experience has affected their lives.

COMMON CORE STANDARDS FOCUS

- Memoir
- Recognize Cause and Effect

LESSON RESOURCES

Plan and Teach

ⓘ Lesson resources are also available on the **Teacher One Stop DVD-ROM** and online at <u>thinkcentral.com</u>.

Lesson Plan and Resource Guide

My First Free Summer
Memoir by Julia Alvarez

Common Core Focus

RI 1 Cite the textual evidence that supports an analysis of what the text says explicitly. **RI 3** Analyze how a text makes connections among individuals, ideas, and events. **L 4b** Use Latin roots as clues to the meaning of a word.

Unless otherwise noted, all resources can be found in the *Resource Manager*.
ⓘ Lesson resources are also available on the **Teacher One Stop DVD-ROM** and online at **thinkcentral.com.** The Student Edition and selected copy masters are available electronically on the ✐ **Student One Stop DVD-ROM.**

Student/Teacher's Edition Pages	Additional Resources CM = Copy Master T = Transparency
Focus and Motivate	
❑ Big Question p. 114	
❑ Author Biography and Background Information p. 115	❑ ⓘ Literature and Reading Center at **thinkcentral.com**
Teach	
❑ Memoir p. 115	
❑ Recognize Cause and Effect p. 115	❑ Recognize Cause and Effect CM— English p. 137, Spanish p. 138 Ⓓ
❑ Vocabulary in Context p. 115	❑ Vocabulary Study CM p. 139 Ⓓ

Ⓓ = Resources for Differentiation

Student/Teacher's Edition Pages	Additional Resources CM = Copy Master T = Transparency
Practice and Apply: Guided Practice	
Selection and Teacher Notes	❏ 🖉 **Audio Anthology CD** Ⓓ
❏ "My First Free Summer," pp. 116–119	❏ Summary CM—English and Spanish p. 133, Haitian Creole and Vietnamese p. 134 Ⓓ
	❏ Reading Fluency CM p. 144
	❏ 📦 **Best Practices Toolkit**
	❏ New Word Analysis p. E8 [T] Ⓓ
	❏ ❶ Audio Summaries at **thinkcentral.com**
Practice and Apply: After Reading	
❏ Selection Questions p. 120	❏ Reading Check CM p. 142
	❏ Memoir CM— English p. 135, Spanish p. 136 Ⓓ
	❏ Question Support CM p. 143 Ⓓ
	❏ Additional Selection Questions p. 128 Ⓓ
	❏ Ideas for Extension p. 129 Ⓓ
❏ Vocabulary Practice p. 121	❏ Vocabulary Practice CM p. 140
❏ Academic Vocabulary in Writing p. 121	❏ Academic Vocabulary CM p. 2
	❏ Additional Academic Vocabulary CM p. 3
❏ Vocabulary Strategy: The Latin Root *dict* p. 121	❏ Vocabulary Strategy CM p. 141
Assess and Reteach	
Assess	❏ **Diagnostic and Selection Tests**
	❏ Selection Tests A, B/C pp. 43–44, 45–46 Ⓓ
	❏ ❶ ThinkCentral Online Assessment
	❏ 🖉 ExamView Test Generator on the **Teacher One Stop DVD-ROM**
Reteach	❏ ❶ Level Up Online Tutorials on **thinkcentral.com**
❏ Cause and Effect	❏ ❶ Reteaching Worksheets on **thinkcentral.com**
❏ Latin Root *dict*	❏ Reading Lesson 7: Recognizing Cause and Effect
	❏ Vocabulary Lesson 10: Latin Roots

Ⓓ = Resources for Differentiation

Additional Selection Questions

Differentiation Use these questions to provide customized practice with
comprehension and critical thinking skills.

Easy

1. **Recall** Why does Alvarez's mother want her to learn English? (*She wants her
to learn the language of the United States, which might bring democracy to the
Dominican Republic.*)

2. *When is it time to* **LEAVE?**
Why do Alvarez's parents want to leave the Dominican Republic? (*A dictator
rules the country, and the situation is becoming more dangerous.*)

Average

3. **Contrast** Based on the details in the selection and what you already know, what
is the difference between a dictatorship and a democracy? What do dictators
require that leaders of democratic societies do not? (*Unlike a democracy,
a dictatorship limits people's rights to travel freely or protest against the
government. To maintain their power, dictators need control of the military and
a strong police force.*)

4. **Analyze Cause and Effect** What are Alvarez's parents afraid will happen
to their family? Why are they worried about this? (*They worry that they will
be arrested by the secret police or soldiers and prevented from leaving the
country. Alvarez's father has been involved in an underground plot against the
government.*)

5. *When is it time to* **LEAVE?**
When her family arrives in the United States, what happens that makes Alvarez
feel like she is home? (*An American official asks if she and her sister are ready
for school. She responds with the same attitude she had when she was in the
Dominican Republic.*)

Challenging

6. *When is it time to* **LEAVE?**
Think about how you would feel if you had to leave your country suddenly.
Which parts of the memoir express your possible sentiments? (*Responses will
probably refer to the parts of the memoir that describe Alvarez's feelings for her
family and friends.*)

7. **Draw Conclusions** The phrase "freedom and liberty and justice for all"
[line 93] is a reference to the Pledge of Allegiance, recited by many American
schoolchildren. What do you think is the significance of its use here? (*Alvarez
becomes aware that her family is escaping to freedom. Writing this later in life,
she might be thinking of having recited the Pledge of Allegiance in American
schools and what it has meant to her.*)

Ideas for Extension

Differentiation These activities provide students with a variety of options for demonstrating understanding of lesson concepts.

EXPLORATIONS AND ACTIVITIES

CREATE TIMELINE: UNDERSTAND SETTING

Have students use information in the textbook and from other sources to create a timeline of the history of the Dominican Republic. Suggest that they illustrate the timeline with photographs and illustrations of important people and events. Invite volunteers to display their timelines.

Pre-AP Challenge: Have students study the history of the island of Hispaniola, including European colonization, independence movements, and 20th century challenges. Half of the students could focus on the Dominican Republic, and the other half could focus on Haiti. Challenge them to explain how the island's geography has influenced its history. Have students compile and present a report, illustrated with a map and other relevant visuals.

ORAL READING: INTERPRET THEME

Explain that Julia Alvarez has written books for children, young adults, and adults. Many of them are set in the Dominican Republic or are related in some way to her experience growing up in that country and also in the United States.

Give students a reading list of Julia Alvarez's work (see her website, www.juliaalvarez.com/about/publications.php). Have them choose one story or several poems from a poetry collection. After they have read their selections, ask them to choose one passage or poem that they think is representative of the collection or story's theme and tone. Invite students to read these aloud in small groups of other students. Then have students discuss the importance and relevance of the passages.

DEBATE: SUPPORT OPINIONS

Explain that the United States and several other countries have intervened in the affairs of various Caribbean nations to ensure political or economic stability.

Divide the class into two groups, and ask students to debate the following questions: Does any country have the right to interfere in the affairs of another country? If so, under what conditions would intervention be acceptable? If not, why not? Encourage students to cite examples from current or historical events to support their positions in the debate.

INQUIRY AND RESEARCH

LEADERS OF THE CARIBBEAN

Tell students that many countries in the Caribbean region, including the Dominican Republic, Haiti, and Cuba, have been led by dictators at times.

Organize small groups, and have each group research a different leader of a Caribbean or Central American country. In addition to Trujillo, they can find information about Cuba's Batista and Castro, Haiti's "Papa Doc" Duvalier and Aristide, and Nicaragua's Somoza. Encourage them to find primary as well as secondary sources, including quotations, newspaper articles and editorials, political cartoons, letters, photographs, and public documents.

Once students have completed their research, have them share what they have learned with the other groups, providing a clear picture of the leader's rise to power and subsequent events. Encourage students to draw comparisons and contrasts among the leaders.

WRITING

EXPLORE GENRE: MEMOIR

Refer students to the journal entry that they wrote during the **QUICKWRITE** activity on page 114. Ask them what other ideas or memories of that experience have arisen during their reading and study of Alvarez's memoir.

Next, invite students to expand their journal entry into a memoir. They might imitate the chronological structure of Alvarez's memoir, or jump back and forth in time. Encourage them to flesh out their account of the experience with details of setting and other people and to incorporate dialogue. Explain that the dialogue does not have to reflect the exact words that were spoken in the past, but that they should try to capture the flavor of the conversation.

ADAPT PLOT: ONE-ACT PLAY

Suggest that students adapt the events of Alvarez's memoir into a one-act play. They may use existing dialogue as well as invent new dialogue, in particular between Alvarez's parents while they are still planning to leave for the United States and then when they are waiting in the airport. Suggest that much of the narrative could be told in monologue form and that there could be two or three short scenes.

Have small groups act out scenes from the plays.

Teacher Notes

Review and Evaluate Outcome
What did I want students to know or be able to do?   How successful was the lesson?

Evaluate Process
What worked? • Strategies   • Resources   • Differentiation   What did not work? Why not?

Reflect
The next time I teach "My First Free Summer," what will I do differently? Why?

Plan Ahead
What must I do next?

Summary

MY FIRST FREE SUMMER
Julia Alvarez
Setting: Dominican Republic, 1960

Julia Alvarez remembers never having a free summer. She attends summer school every year because she doesn't see the point of learning to speak English. Her mother wants her daughter to learn English to prepare for political liberation of the Dominican Republic by the U.S. Alvarez's father is, in fact, involved in an underground plot to help liberate the country from its dictatorship.

At school Alvarez finally decides to concentrate, and she does win freedom from summer school. By this time, however, the friends and relatives she counted on as companions are fleeing to the United States. Secret police and massive arrests terrorize her family. One day, her mother announces that their papers and tickets have arrived. They are leaving for the United States.

MI PRIMER VERANO LIBRE
Julia Alvarez
Setting: Dominican Republic, 1960

Julia Alvarez recuerda nunca haber tenido un verano libre. Ella asiste a la escuela de verano cada año porque no ve el caso de aprender a hablar inglés. Su madre quiere que su hija aprenda inglés para prepararse para la liberación política de la República Dominicana por parte de los Estados Unidos. El padre de Alvarez, de hecho, está involucrado en una conspiración para liberar al país de su dictador.

En la escuela, Alvarez finalmente decide concentrarse y logra liberarse de la escuela de verano. Sin embargo, para entonces los amigos y los parientes con los que contaba como compañeros están huyendo a los Estados Unidos. La policía secreta y los arrestos masivos aterrorizan a su familia. Un día, su madre anuncia que sus papeles y sus boletos han llegado. Se van a los Estados Unidos.

Summary

PREMYE LETE LIB MWEN
Julia Alvarez
Espas ak tan: Repiblik Dominikèn, 1960

Jilya Alvarèz sonje li pa janm pase yon lete lib. Li ale nan lekòl lete chak ane paske li pa wè enpòtans sa genyen pou l aprann pale Angle. Manman an vle pou pitit fi li aprann Angle pou l prepare pou liberasyon politik Repiblik Dominikèn gras a Etazini. Papa Alvarèz fè pati konplo sekrè k ap fèt pou ede libere peyi a nan diktati li ye a.

Nan lekòl la, Alvarez deside konsantre l finalman sou etid angle, epi li vin jwenn libète li pou l ale nan vakans lete li. Men, nan moman sa a, zanmi ak manm fanmi li te konte sou yo pou sèvi l konpayon, tout ale Ozetazini. Lapolis sekrè ak anpil arestasyon k ap fèt vin lakòz fanmi li gen anpil laperèz. Yon jou, manman li anonse papye yo ak tikè yo rive. Y ap kite peyi a pou yo ale Ozetazini.

Mùa hè Tự do Đầu tiên của Tôi
Julia Alvarez
Bối cảnh: Cộng hòa Dominica, 1960

Julia Alvarez nhớ không bao giờ có mùa hè tự do. Bà phải học hè hàng năm vì bà không thấy mục đích trong việc học nói tiếng Anh. Mẹ bà muốn con gái mình học tiếng Anh để chuẩn bị cho việc giải phóng chính trị của của nước Mỹ đối với Cộng hòa Dominica. Thực tế, cha của Alvarez tham gia vào một kế hoạch bí mật để giúp giải phóng đất nước khỏi chế độ độc tài của nó.

Cuối cùng Alvarez quyết định tập trung học ở trường, và bà đã thoát khỏi kỳ học hè. Tuy nhiên vào thời điểm này, các bạn và những người họ hàng mà bà có thể tin tưởng làm bạn lại bỏ đi Mỹ. Cảnh sát mật và sự bắt bớ hàng loạt đe dọa gia đình bà. Một hôm, mẹ bà thông báo rằng giấy tờ và vé của họ đã đến. Họ lên đường đi Mỹ.

MY FIRST FREE SUMMER

Text Analysis

MEMOIR

A **memoir** is a form of autobiographical writing in which a writer describes important events in his or her life. Most memoirs

- use the first–person point of view
- are true accounts of actual events
- describe conflicts faced by the writer
- include the writer's feelings about historical events or social issues

Directions: In the chart, record some of Julia Alvarez's personal experiences and some of the historical events from the memoir. An example has been done for you.

Personal Experiences	Historical Events
	"For thirty years, the Dominican Republic had endured a bloody and repressive dictatorship." (lines 7–8)

SPANISH

MY FIRST FREE SUMMER   COPY MASTER

Text Analysis

MEMOIR

Una **memoria** es una forma de escrito autobiográfico en la cual el escritor describe acontecimientos importantes de su vida. La mayoría de las memorias:

- usan el punto de vista de la primera persona.
- son relatos verdaderos de acontecimientos reales.
- describen conflictos que el escritor enfrentó.
- incluyen los sentimientos del escritor sobre acontecimientos históricos o temas sociales.

Instrucciones: En la gráfica, anota algunas de las experiencias personales de Julia Alvarez y algunos de los acontecimientos históricos de la memoria. Sigue el ejemplo.

Experiencias personales	Eventos históricos
	"For thirty years, the Dominican Republic had endured a bloody and repressive dictatorship." (líneas 7–8)

MY FIRST FREE SUMMER

Reading Skill

RECOGNIZE CAUSE AND EFFECT

Events are often related by **cause and effect,** which means that one event brings
about the other. The first event is the **cause,** and what follows is the effect.
Sometimes, one cause can have many effects. Recognizing cause and effect
relationships can help you understand important turning points, because you'll be
aware of the consequences of events and actions.

Directions: In the chart, record effects that the political struggle in Alvarez's
homeland had on her life.

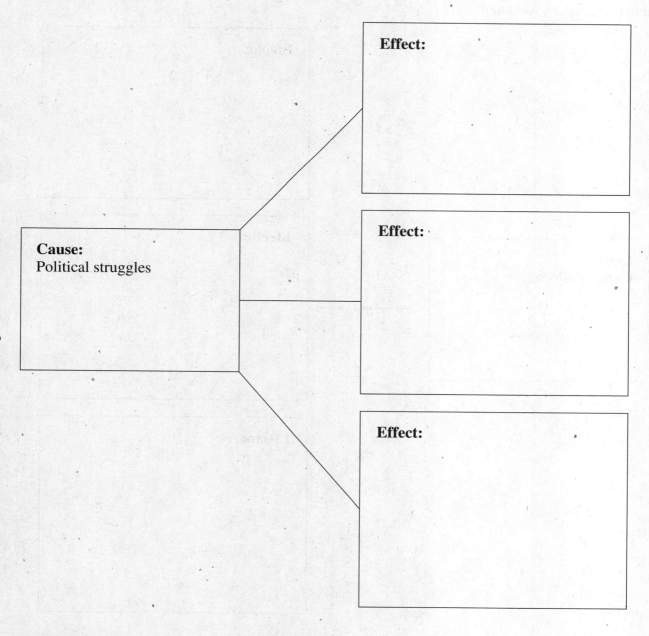

Effect:

Effect:

Cause:
Political struggles

Effect:

MI PRIMER VERANO LIBRE

Reading Skill

RECOGNIZE CAUSE AND EFFECT

Los acontecimientos con frecuencia se relacionan por **causa y efecto,** lo cual significa que un acontecimiento produce al otro. El primer acontecimiento es la **causa,** y lo que lo sigue es el efecto. A veces, una causa puede tener varios efectos. Reconocer relaciones de causa y efecto puede ayudarte a entender momentos decisivos, porque estarás consciente de las consecuencias de los acontecimientos y de las acciones.

Instrucciones: En la gráfica, anota los efectos que las luchas políticas en su tierra natal tuvieron en Alvarez.

Efecto:

Causa:
Luchas políticas

Efecto:

Efecto:

MY FIRST FREE SUMMER

Vocabulary Study

VOCABULARY IN CONTEXT

Directions: As your teacher reads each item, listen for the boldfaced word. Discuss possible meanings of the word, and write on the chart what you think the word means. After reading "My First Free Summer," confirm or adjust your definitions.

1. In a **contradiction** of her opponent's claim that the food in the school cafeteria is unhealthy, Reba said, "I disagree. Students now have the option of eating salads and other healthy foods. We should focus on other issues in the campaign for student body president."

2. After Jonah broke the window playing basketball indoors, he received an intense **interrogation** from his parents, who demanded to know what he had been thinking.

3. The reservoir was **replete** with water after the heavy rains.

4. The dog trainer is able to **summon** my dog quite easily, but I can't get her to come to me no matter how many times I call.

5. At first it seemed that the case against the thief was very tight, but detail by detail, it began to **unravel.**

Vocabulary Word	Predicted Meaning	Meaning in Selection
1. contradiction		
2. interrogation		
3. replete		
4. summon		
5. unravel		

Vocabulary Practice

contradiction	replete	unravel	interrogation	summon

A. Directions: Write the word from the box that correctly completes each sentence.

1. Mrs. Forsythe's new kitchen is _____ with all the latest gadgets.

2. A deposition is a pre-trial _____, or questioning, of a witness that is usually held in a lawyer's office.

3. Tony wanted to _____ the mystery before he read the final chapter.

4. A paradox is a seeming _____ that, in fact, reveals some truth.

5. The lawyer needed to _____ more witnesses in order to make his case stronger.

B. Directions: Circle the word in each group that is the same or almost the same in meaning as the **boldfaced** word.

6. **unravel**
   undo   unlock   unburden   unhinge

7. **replete**
   bright   lavish   wasteful   round

8. **summon**
   groan   extend   call   surrender

9. **contradiction**
   gadget   hope   contract   denial

10. **interrogation**
    reading   questioning   research   interruption

C. Writing Option: Write a short paragraph about how you think Julia Alvarez settled into America. Use at least two words from the box.

_____

_____

_____

MY FIRST FREE SUMMER

Vocabulary Strategy

THE LATIN ROOT *dict*

The vocabulary word *contradiction* contains the Latin root *dict* (also spelled *dic*), which means "say" or "speak." Your understanding of this root can help you to figure out the meaning of other words formed from *dict*.

abdicate	edict	benediction	indicate
contradict	indictment	dedicate	jurisdiction

A. Directions: Fill in each blank with the correct word from the box.

1. The FBI in Washington, D.C., has _____ to investigate federal crimes.

2. The actor will _____ his performance in the play to his family.

3. The grand jury issued an _____ charging the felon with bank robbery.

4. Our teacher distributed an _____ listing the rules on how to submit our essays.

5. The citizens did not ask the king to _____ his throne.

6. The results of the experiment _____ the scientist's theory.

7. After the service, the clergyman gave a _____.

8. We created a set of rules to _____ the guidelines for our club.

B. Directions: Select any four words from the box and write an original sentence for each one.

_____

_____

_____

_____

_____

_____

MY FIRST FREE SUMMER

Reading Check

Directions: Recall the events in Julia Alvarez's memoir. Then answer the questions in phrases or sentences.

1. Why did Julia Alvarez's mother decide to send her children to American school?

_____

_____

_____

2. Why was Alvarez jealous of her friends who attended Dominican schools?

_____

_____

_____

3. Why did Alvarez become a better student in fifth grade?

_____

_____

_____

4. What did Alvarez realize as she sat in the airport with her parents, waiting for the plane to take them to the United States?

_____

_____

_____

5. What did Alvarez fear as the U.S. official reviewed her family's documents?

_____

_____

_____

MY FIRST FREE SUMMER

Question Support

TEXT ANALYSIS

For questions 1–2, see page 120 of the Student Edition.

Directions: Answer the questions.

3. **Interpret Memoir** List two possible meanings of the word "free" that can be found in the memoir.

_____

_____

_____

4. **Analyze Personality Traits** Describe one way in which Julia Alvarez changes from the beginning of the story to the end.

_____

_____

_____

5. **Analyze Perspective** The memoir is written by an adult from a child's point of view. Describe one detail that lets you know this selection is written by an adult.

_____

_____

_____

6. **Generalize About Cause and Effect** Describe one effect that political struggle had on Alvarez.

_____

_____

_____

MY FIRST FREE SUMMER

Reading Fluency

READING WITH EXPRESSION

To make any piece of literature come alive for your listeners, you must read with expression. To read with expression means to read with feeling and emotion. Here are some tips for making your reading more expressive.

- Read at a natural pace, or speed. Speed up or slow down as necessary. Avoid reading word-by word.
- Change the volume of your voice to signal that a word or idea is important.
- Vary the pitch of your voice, making it rise and fall, to create a conversational tone and avoid sounding dull.
- Group words into meaningful phrases. Pause or stop to signal the end of a thought or idea.

Directions: Follow along as your teacher reads this passage about summer jobs. Listen for changes in the volume and pitch of your teacher's voice. Notice where your teacher pauses or stops. Then use these marks to prepare your own reading of the passage:

L = louder	↑ = raise pitch	/ = pause or stop
S = softer	↓ = lower pitch	underscore = add stress

While summer brings time for freedom and relaxation, it also brings time for enriching and rewarding new experiences. About half of all students between 16 and 24 work each summer. A summer job can mean opportunities for financial gain as well as personal growth.

Most young people who have summer jobs use them to save money for various expenses, such as education. Yet earning money is not the only reason to get a summer job. A job can provide opportunities to learn new skills and to meet new people. It might even give you a chance to see the world.

For example, each year some students take jobs on the fishing ships that sail the Alaskan coast. Other students wait tables in summer resorts areas like Cape Cod, Massachusetts. And hundreds of students find jobs each year in Washington D.C., working for some branch of the federal government. A few lucky people even find jobs that take them to other countries. They might work in France, China, Peru, or Mali.

So think long and hard about what you will do this summer. What you do could change your life. (189 words).

THE GREAT RatHunt

Laurence Yep

WHY THIS SELECTION?

Laurence Yep is an accomplished Chinese-American writer of young-adult literature. Students will appreciate Yep's vivid description of his childhood experiences.

ABOUT THIS SELECTION

Student/Teacher's Edition Pages: 122–135
Difficulty Level: Easy
Readability Scores: Lexile 650; Fry: 4; Dale-Chall: 6.0

Summary Having asthma means that the young Laurence Yep isn't able to play sports with his father and brother. Because of this, Yep believes he is a disappointment to his father. In a revealing conversation between Yep and his father, Yep learns that his father had to overcome fear and hardship as a new immigrant from China. Yep also learns that his value is not determined by his athletic ability.

Engaging the Students This memoir provides students with the opportunity to examine their thoughts about fear and when it's appropriate to be scared. When his father asks him to help catch a rat that has invaded their apartment, Yep learns that everyone, even the father he idealizes, is scared at times.

COMMON CORE STANDARDS FOCUS

• Conflict in Nonfiction
• Identify Chronological Order

LESSON RESOURCES
Plan and Teach

Student Copy Masters

ℹ Lesson resources are also available on the **Teacher One Stop** DVD-ROM and online at <u>thinkcentral.com</u>.

Copyright © Holt McDougal, a division of Houghton Mifflin Harcourt

Lesson Plan and Resource Guide

The Great Rat Hunt
Memoir by Laurence Yep

Common Core Focus

RI 3 Analyze how a text makes connections among individuals, ideas, and events. **RI 5** Analyze the structure of a text. **W 2** Write explanatory texts. **L 1** Demonstrate command of standard English grammar when writing. **L 4a** Use context (e.g., a word's position or function in a sentence) as a clue to the meaning of a word. **L 5b** Use the relationship between words to better understand each of the words.

Unless otherwise noted, all resources can be found in the *Resource Manager*.
🛈 Lesson resources are also available on the **Teacher One Stop DVD-ROM** and online at **thinkcentral.com**. The Student Edition and selected copy masters are available electronically on the 💿 **Student One Stop DVD-ROM.**

Student/Teacher's Edition Pages	Additional Resources CM = Copy Master T = Transparency
Focus and Motivate	
❏ Big Question p. 122	
❏ Author Biography p. 123	❏ 🛈 Literature and Reading Center at **thinkcentral.com**
Teach	
❏ Conflict in Nonfiction p. 123	
❏ Identify Chronological Order p. 123	❏ Identify Chronological Order CM— English p. 157, Spanish p. 158 🄳
❏ Vocabulary in Context p. 123	❏ Vocabulary Study CM p. 159 🄳
Practice and Apply: Guided Practice	
Selection and Teacher Notes ❏ "The Great Rat Hunt," pp. 124–132	❏ 💿 **Audio Anthology CD** 🄳 ❏ Summary CM—English and Spanish p. 153, Haitian Creole and Vietnamese p. 154 🄳 ❏ Reading Fluency CM p. 165 ❏ 🧰 **Best Practices Toolkit** ❏ Think-Pair-Share p. A18 [T] 🄳 ❏ Monitoring p. A12 [T] 🄳 ❏ 🛈 Audio Summaries at **thinkcentral.com**

🄳 = Resources for Differentiation

Student/Teacher's Edition Pages	Additional Resources CM = Copy Master T = Transparency

Practice and Apply: After Reading

❑ Selection Questions p. 133	❑ Reading Check CM p. 162 ❑ Conflict in Nonfiction CM— English p. 155, Spanish p. 156 ⒟ ❑ Question Support CM p. 163 ⒟ ❑ Additional Selection Questions p. 148 ⒟ ❑ Ideas for Extension p. 149 ⒟
❑ Vocabulary Practice p. 134 ❑ Academic Vocabulary in Speaking p. 134 ❑ Vocabulary Strategy: Context Clues p. 134	❑ Vocabulary Practice CM p. 160 ❑ Academic Vocabulary CM p. 2 ❑ Additional Academic Vocabulary CM p. 3 ❑ Vocabulary Strategy CM p. 161 ❑ ⓘ *WordSharp* Interactive Vocabulary Tutor **DVD-ROM** and online at **thinkcentral.com**
❑ Grammar in Context p. 135 ❑ Writing Prompt p. 135	❑ Use Past Perfect Tense Correctly CM p. 164 ❑ Grammar Handbook—Student Edition p. R53

Assess and Reteach

Assess	❑ **Diagnostic and Selection Tests** ❑ Selection Tests A, B/C pp. 47–48, 49–50 ⒟ ❑ ⓘ ThinkCentral Online Assessment ❑ ✐ ExamView Test Generator on the **Teacher One Stop DVD-ROM**

Reteach
❑ Conflict in Nonfiction
❑ Context Clues
❑ Chronological Order
❑ Past Perfect Tense
	❑ ⓘ Level Up Online Tutorials on **thinkcentral.com**
	❑ ⓘ Reteaching Worksheets on **thinkcentral.com**
	  ❑ Literature Lesson 6: Conflict
	  ❑ Vocabulary Lesson 13: Context Clues: Definition and Restatement
	  ❑ Vocabulary Lesson 14: Context Clues: Comparison and Contrast
	  ❑ Reading Lesson 6: Recognizing Sequence and Chronological Order
	  ❑ Grammar Lesson 16: Basic Verb Tenses

⒟ = Resources for Differentiation

THE GREAT RAT HUNT

Additional Selection Questions

Use to supplement the questions on SE page 133.

Differentiation Use these questions to provide customized practice with comprehension and critical thinking skills.

Easy

1. ***When is it OK to be SCARED?***
What does Yep's father say to show how scared he was when he came to America? (*He says, "'They had to pry my fingers from the boat railing'"* [*line 242*].)

2. **Recall Conflict** What conflict does Yep reveal at the beginning of the memoir? (*Because of his asthma, he can't play sports like his brother and father.*)

3. **Recall Conflict** What is the conflict between Yep's mother and father? (*She doesn't want him to use a rifle to shoot the rat.*)

Average

4. **Examine Conflict** Name an example of a conflict from Yep's father's life. (*In lines 138–148, Yep's father tells how when he first came to America he "'got beaten up by the white kids. And when the white kids weren't around, there were the other Chinese kids. . . . they like to give a China-born a hard time.'"*)

5. **Understand Chronological Order** With a partner, take turns retelling the events of the text in your own words. Refer to the chart that you filled in as you read the story. (*Students should use the charts they made while reading to cover the major events in chronological order.*)

6. **Analyze Conflict** How is the conflict between Yep and his father resolved? (*After working together to catch the rat, and talking, Yep begins to see his father more realistically and also realizes that his father accepts him for who he is.*)

Challenging

7. ***When is it OK to be SCARED?***
Although Yep is scared, he agrees to help his father hunt the rat. Why might people do something frightening despite their fear? (*People do things even when they're scared if something else, such as approval from a parent, is important. Yep felt he had to prove himself to his father, so he overlooked his fear to help his father hunt the rat.*)

8. **Examine Characterization** Name some ways that Yep uses his father's words and actions to explain his father's character. (*Yep shows that his father is gruff when his father grunts and says, "'Here. Open this'"* [*line 118*]. *Yep shows that his father has a sense of humor when he makes the trophy for the rat.*)

Ideas for Extension

Differentiation These activities provide students with a variety of options for demonstrating understanding of lesson concepts.

EXPLORATIONS AND ACTIVITIES

PERFORM: EXPLORE CHARACTER AND CONFLICT

In this memoir, Yep characterizes his family members through their words and actions. Invite students to choose a scene from the memoir to perform dramatically. They may work in pairs or small groups. Ask them to use voice and gesture to convey the drama of the scene.

After each performance, ask the students to discuss any conflicts portrayed in the scene and their reasons for performing that particular scene. Ask them to describe the character traits of the person they were portraying.

GRAPHIC TIMELINE: USE CHRONOLOGICAL ORDER

Have students create a timeline of the major events in the memoir using words and pictures to show how one event leads to another.

After students have finished their timelines, discuss the point at which the climax took place. What happened after the climax?

CARTOON STRIP: INTERPRET PLOT AND SEQUENCE

Invite students to draw a cartoon strip humorously depicting the scene in which Yep and his father wait for the rat and then run from the room. Students might choose to draw the strip from the rat's point of view, showing the man and boy peering into the hole and then running out of the room in fear. If they choose, students can include speech bubbles with important dialogue from the memoir.

After students have completed their cartoon strips, create a space on the wall to display their work.

VENN DIAGRAM: COMPARE AND CONTRAST CHARACTERS

Ask small groups of students to create a Venn diagram comparing and contrasting Yep and his brother Eddy. Then have the students create a dialogue between Yep and Eddy that illustrates their characters. The scene may be dramatic or humorous. It can be based on actual events from the memoir or on imagined events.

Have each group act out its dialogue. Then lead the class in a discussion about the differences they observed between the characters.

POSTER: EXAMINE CONFLICT AND RESOLUTION

Have students identify something they are good at, such as a sport, craft, or musical instrument. Encourage them to think about the challenges and difficulties they had to overcome to become as skilled as they are.

Students should then create a poster showing their chosen talent with an explanation of it. Have them include challenges they faced as they were learning their skills. Students should use words and illustrations. Ask students to present their posters to the class.

INQUIRY AND RESEARCH

CHINESE IMMIGRANTS

Divide the class into small groups and have each group do research on the history of Chinese immigrants in America. Students may research why immigrants came to America, what they did when they arrived, where and how they lived, and their legacy. Have each group prepare a report on their subject, including illustrations or photographs, if possible, and the sources they used.

Pre-AP Challenge: Have students research challenges that recent immigrants to the United States face. Have them discuss their findings, and suggest ways that U.S. citizens can help recent immigrants adjust to their new lives.

WRITING

SUMMARIZE PLOT: JOURNAL ENTRY

Have students write a journal entry as if they were Laurence Yep writing in his journal the night after the rat hunt. Students should recap the events of the day. They should also include their feelings about how the events worked out.

IDENTIFY CONFLICT AND RESOLUTION: PERSONAL ESSAY

Ask students to write a three-paragraph essay about a time when they felt like an outsider, keeping in mind these questions: What was the event or situation? Why did they feel the way they did? What did they do to come to terms with the challenges they faced?

Teacher Notes

Review and Evaluate Outcome
What did I want students to know or be able to do?   How successful was the lesson?

Evaluate Process
What worked? • Strategies   • Resources   • Differentiation   What did not work? Why not?

Reflect
The next time I teach "The Great Rat Hunt," what will I do differently? Why?

Plan Ahead
What must I do next?

THE GREAT RAT HUNT

Summary

THE GREAT RAT HUNT
Laurence Yep
Setting: San Francisco, California, 20th Century

When Laurence Yep was a boy, he had asthma, which made it hard for him to breathe. It was impossible for him to play sports with his father and brother. He felt left out and thought his father considered him a failure. A rat is found in the Yeps's store, and Mr. Yeps calls an exterminator. When the rat makes its way to the family house to escape the poisonous chemicals, Mr. Yep borrows a rifle and asks his sons to help. Laurence agrees to help right away, but his brother refuses. Although they never do shoot the rat, hunting it together gives Laurence a different feeling about his father.

LA GRAN CACERÍA DE LA RATA
Laurence Yep
Escenario: San Francisco, California, siglo XX

Cuando Laurence Yep era niño, tenía asma, lo que le dificultaba respirar. Para él era imposible jugar deportes con su padre y su hermano. Se sentía segregado y pensaba que su papá lo consideraba un fracasado. Un día, una rata aparece en la tienda de los Yep y el Sr. Yep llama al exterminador. Cuando la rata se abre camino dentro de la casa de la familia para escapar de los químicos venenosos, el Sr. Yep pide prestado un rifle y les pide a sus hijos que le ayuden. Laurence acepta ayudar de inmediato, pero su hermano se rehusa. A pesar de que nunca le disparan a la rata, cazarla juntos le da a Laurence un sentimiento diferente con respecto de su padre.

Summary

LACHAS DÈYÈ GWO RAT LA

Laurence Yep

Espas ak tan : San Fransisko, Kalifòni, 20^{yèm} Syèk

Lè Lòrenns Yèp te yon ti gason, li te gen opresyon, e sa te fè li difisil pou li respire. Li te enposib pou li jwe jwèt espò avèk papa l ak frè li. Li santi yo mete l sou kote epi li panse papa li konsidere li kòm yon echèk. Yo jwenn yon rat nan magazen Yèp yo, epi Msye Yèp rele yon ekstèminatè. Lè rat la sove pou li ale nan kay fanmi an pou l ka chape anba pwodui chimik pwazon an, Msye Yèp prete yon fizi epi li mande pitit gason li yo pou ede li. Lòrenns dakò pou ede li touswit, men frè li a refize. Menm si yo pa janm tire rat la, lachas yo fè dèyè li ansanm nan fè Lòrenns vin gen yon santiman diferan sou papa li.

Cuộc Săn Chuột Tuyệt vời

Laurence Yep

Bối cảnh: San Francisco, California, Thế kỷ 20

Khi Laurence Yep còn nhỏ, cậu bị hen, bệnh hen làm cậu khó thở. Cậu không thể chơi thể thao với bố và anh trai của cậu. Cậu cảm thấy bị ra rìa và nghĩ rằng bố cậu coi cậu như một sự thất bại. Người ta tìm thấy một con chuột cống ở trong kho nhà Yeps và ông Yeps gọi một người diệt chuột đến. Khi con chuột tìm đường chạy vào trong nhà để chốn thoát hóa chất độc này, ông Yep mượn khẩu súng trường và bảo các con trai ông giúp đỡ. Laurence đồng ý giúp ngay, nhưng anh cậu thì từ chối. Mặc dù không bao giờ họ bắn chuột cả, nhưng cùng nhau đuổi bắt nó đem lại cho Laurence một tình cảm khác về cha mình.

THE GREAT RAT HUNT

COPY MASTER

Text Analysis

CONFLICT IN NONFICTION

In this memoir, Lauren Yep relates an event from childhood. To tell this real-life
story, he uses some of the same literary elements that appear in his fiction. For
example, the narrative centers around **conflicts**, or struggles between opposing
forces.

Directions: In the conflict map, record only one of the selection's most important
conflicts and the events that lead to its resolution, or outcome.

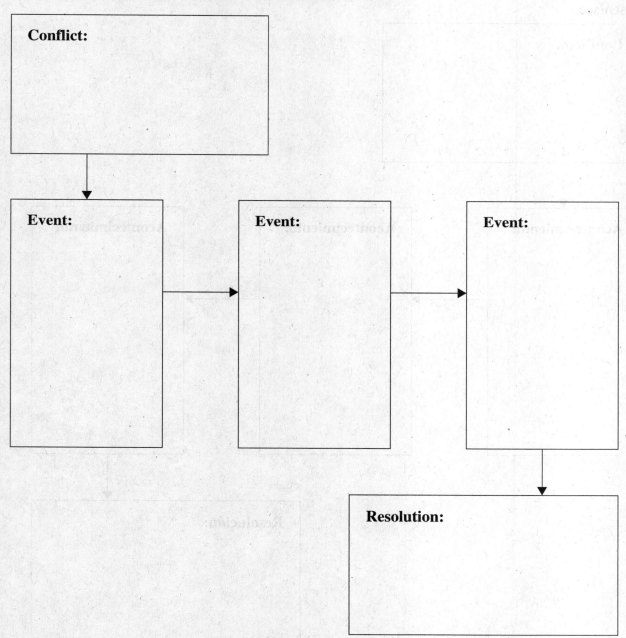

Conflict:

Event:

Event:

Event:

Resolution:

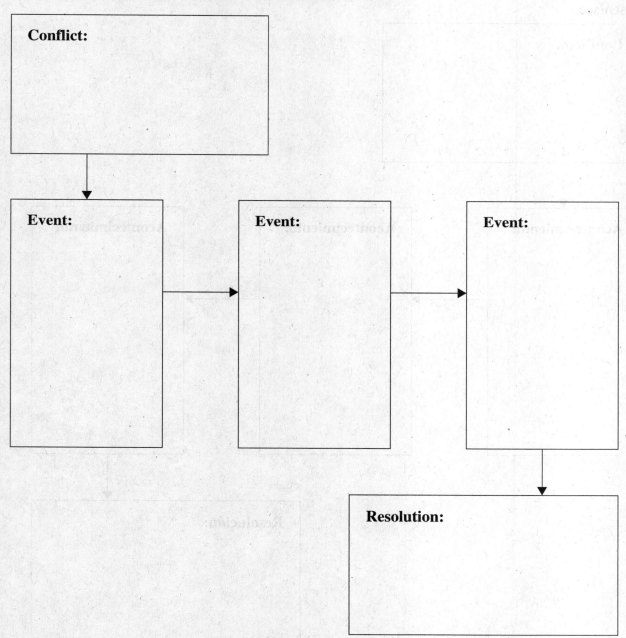
THE GREAT RAT HUNT

Text Analysis

CONFLICT IN NONFICTION

En esta memoria, Lauren Yep relata un acontecimiento de su niñez. Para narrar este relato de la vida real, él usa algunos de los mismos elementos literarios que aparecen en su ficción. Por ejemplo, la narrativa se centra alrededor de los conflictos, o las luchas entre las fuerzas opuestas.

Instrucciones: En el mapa de **conflicto**, anota sólo uno de los conflictos más importantes de la selección y los acontecimientos que llevan a su **resolución** o desenlace.

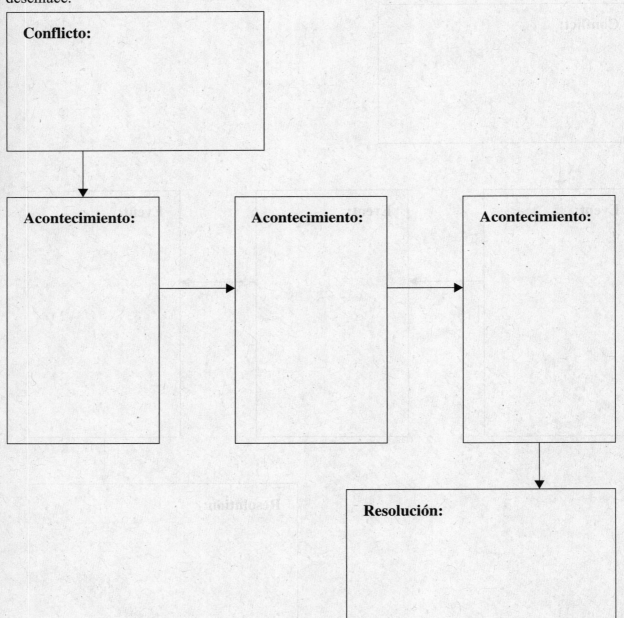

Conflicto:

Acontecimiento:

Acontecimiento:

Acontecimiento:

Resolución:

SPANISH

THE GREAT RAT HUNT   COPY MASTER

Reading Skill

IDENTIFY CHRONOLOGICAL ORDER

Memoirs are often organized in **chronological order,** which means that events are presented in the order in which they happened. To make sure you know when each event occurs, follow these steps:

- Identify individual events taking place.
- Look for words and phrases that signal order, such as: *before, after, first, next, then, while, the next day, an hour and a half later*

Directions: In the chart, record key events in order, using parallel boxes when two actions occur at the same time. An example has been done for you.

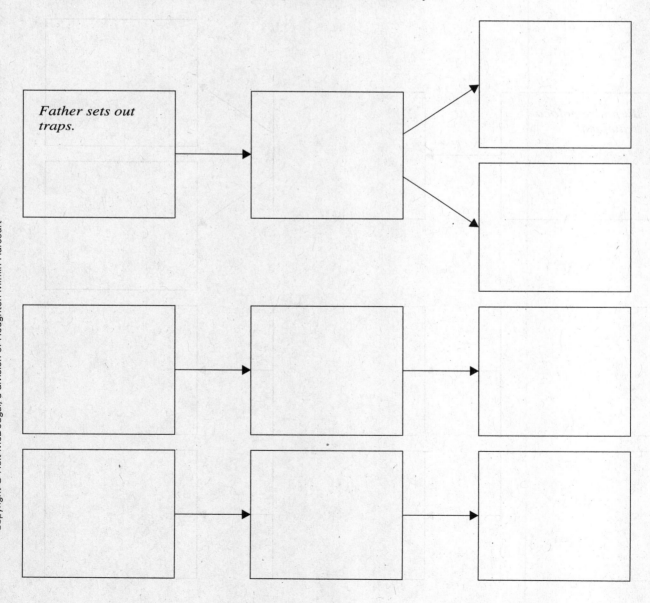

Father sets out traps.

LA GRAN CACERÍA DE LA RATA

Reading Skill

IDENTIFY CHRONOLOGICAL ORDER

Las memorias con frecuencia se organizan en **orden cronológico,** lo que significa que los acontecimientos se presentan en el orden en el cual sucedieron. Para asegurarte de que sabes cuándo ocurre cada acontecimiento, sigue estos pasos.

- Identifica los acontecimientos individuales que tienen lugar.
- Busca palabras y frases que señalan orden como: *antes, después, primero, siguiente, entonces, mientras, al día siguiente, una hora y media después.*

Direcciones: En la tabla, anota en orden los acontecimientos clave, usando cuadros paralelos cuando ocurren dos acciones al mismo tiempo. Sigue el ejemplo.

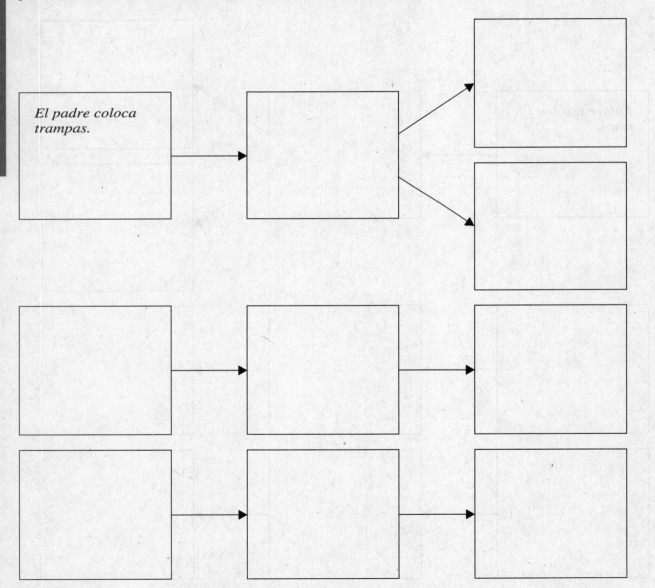

El padre coloca trampas.

THE GREAT RAT HUNT   COPY MASTER

Vocabulary Study

VOCABULARY IN CONTEXT

barricade	improvised	perpetual	ravage	vigilant
brusquely	ineptitude	rationalize	reserve	wince

A. Directions: As your teacher reads each sentence, listen for the boldfaced word. Then discuss the possible meaning of the word.

1. The cars couldn't get past the **barricade** built across the street.

2. The rude clerk **brusquely** hurried me through the line.

3. Joey **improvised** because he hadn't prepared a speech.

4. As if to advertise my **ineptitude,** I tripped on the stairs on the way to the stage.

5. "I hate this game!" Tom whined. "Am I doomed to be the **perpetual** loser?"

6. I can **rationalize** having dessert if I don't eat fries with dinner.

7. The forest fire will **ravage** anything in its path.

8. She let go of her usual **reserve** and yelled wildly.

9. My mother reminded me to be **vigilant** if I walked home after dark.

10. As I pulled the bandage off, I saw him **wince.**

THE GREAT RAT HUNT

Resource Manager

THE GREAT RAT HUNT   COPY MASTER

Vocabulary Practice

barricade	perpetual	vigilant	ineptitude	reserve
improvised	ravage	brusquely	rationalize	wince

A. Directions: Write the word from the box that correctly completes each sentence.

1. The _____ caused by the tornado destroyed the town.

2. Marti, April, and Faye _____ a skit for the school talent show.

3. Mr. Harris responded to my question _____ and quickly, which frightened me.

4. Keira's quiet _____ makes many people think she is shy.

5. I _____ every time I hear Mr. Samuels say a word with many syllables.

6. Karen is always misbehaving in class, so we think of her as a _____ nuisance.

7. Juan is trying to _____ his need for a new computer to his parents.

8. Because I have an _____ with numbers, I do not get high grades in math.

9. The rebels placed a _____ in front of the entrance to the fort.

10. The guard was _____ as he checked every visitor carefully.

B. Directions: For each word in the first column, find the word in the second column that is closest in meaning. Write the letter of that phrase in the blank.

_____ 1. brusquely

_____ 2. ineptitude

_____ 3. rationalize

_____ 4. perpetual

_____ 5. reserve

a. demure

b. justify

c. shortcoming

d. bluntly

e. constant

THE GREAT RAT HUNT
Vocabulary Strategy

CONTEXT CLUES

Context clues are words and phrases in a text that suggest the definition of an unfamiliar word. For example, an author might restate or define an unfamiliar word, as in this sentence: It was a farcical, ridiculous idea. An author might also compare an unfamiliar word to something that is familiar: The workers were as expendable as week-old newspaper.

Directions: Use context clues in each sentence to help you determine the meaning of the underlined word. Then underline the clues that helped you figure out the meaning of each word.

1. He had a **voracious** appetite, and he couldn't keep from asking for another serving of food.

   _____

2. Lisa's room is **unkempt** most of the time, and the mess drives her mother crazy.

   _____

3. Our teacher has a way of **galvanizing** her students, and she inspires them to reach their goals.

   _____

4. We were shocked when we found out that our business was **annexed**, taken over unexpectedly.

   _____

5. Just as a child is naturally attracted to candy, Steve has an **affinity** for sports cars.

   _____

THE GREAT RAT HUNT   COPY MASTER

Reading Check

Directions: Recall all characters and events in the story. Then answer each question
in sentences or phrases.

1. How does Yep feel when he watches his father and brother play sports outside? What games
   does he play?

   _____

   _____

   _____

2. At the beginning of the story, how does Yep usually interpret his father's silence?

   _____

   _____

   _____

3. Part of Yep doesn't want to go on the rat hunt. Why does he volunteer to go?

   _____

   _____

   _____

4. Why does Yep begin to feel more comfortable while he and his father wait for the rat?

   _____

   _____

   _____

5. What does Yep's father say when Yep confesses that he's lousy at sports? What does Yep
   learn about his father and about himself as a result of this conversation?

   _____

   _____

   _____

   _____

THE GREAT RAT HUNT

Question Support

TEXT ANALYSIS

For questions 1–3, see page 133 in the Student Edition.

Directions: Answer the questions.

4. **Identify Chronological Order** Complete the sentence.

   The event that takes place right before Father runs out of the apartment is _____

   _____

5. **Examine Conflict** Describe a conflict in the memoir. Then describe the events that lead to its resolution.

   _____

   _____

   _____

6. **Analyze Characters** Why does Yep agree to help his father capture the rat?

   _____

   _____

   _____

7. **Compare and Contrast** Complete the following sentences.

   At the beginning of the memoir, Yep feels _____

   _____

   At the end of the memoir, Yep learns _____

   _____

8. **Interpret Meaning** Reread lines 269–271. Then complete the sentence.

   The word "our" in "our trophy" refers to _____

   _____

COPY MASTER

Grammar in Context

USE PAST PERFECT TENSE CORRECTLY

The tense of a verb indicates the time of the action or the state of being. There are six verb tenses, each expressing a range of time. The past perfect tense shows that an action or condition in the past came before another past action or condition.

Example: She had decided not to go, so he sailed without her.

To form the past perfect tense, combine the verb had with the past participle.

Directions: For each sentence, make the order of events as clear as possible by choosing the best tense of the verb in parentheses.

1. At the beginning of the year, she (studies, had studied) every night of the week.

2. After training all summer, Jason (felt, had felt) he was ready to compete.

3. Angela (searches, had searched) on the school web site several times, but she never noticed her photo.

4. George (practices, had practiced) with the band on Thursday nights.

5. I met my father for the first time, and I (realized, had realized) how much I needed him in my life.

THE GREAT RAT HUNT   COPY MASTER

Reading Fluency

REPEATED READINGS

To get the most from your reading, it helps to read a passage several times. As you read, group words into meaningful phrases that sound like natural speech. Vary the rise and fall of your voice to emphasize important words or ideas. Do not read too fast or too slow.

Directions to the Reader:

1. In a normal voice, practice reading the passage about Chinatown.
2. Then read the passage aloud four times as your checker listens.
3. Evaluate the results.

Directions to the Checker:

1. Follow along while your partner reads, timing the reading. Underline each word the reader mispronounces or skips. Jot down words he or she adds.
2. Check the marked words with the reader. Record them in the chart. Talk about ways he or she can do better.
3. Erase the marks on the passage and repeat these steps three more times.

Reading	1	2	3	4
Total Reading Time				
Words Missed				

While there are hundreds of Chinatowns across the United States, the Chinatown in San Francisco is the largest and the oldest in the nation.

In the mid-1800s, many Chinese immigrants arrived in California to work on the railroads and as mine workers or prospectors during the Gold Rush of 1849. San Francisco's Chinatown became a place where they could find support and feel at home. Soon a law was passed that said people of Chinese ancestry had to live in certain areas. Another law said Chinese children could only go to certain schools. So, many people moved to the area known as Chinatown. As a result Chinatown became a center of Chinese culture, trade, and banking.

Chinatown was completely destroyed in the earthquake of 1906. Some city planners hoped to move Chinatown to a different neighborhood or even to abolish it altogether. Their efforts failed, and Chinatown was rebuilt. Today it is an exciting place where people can experience and learn about Chinese culture.

Paul Revere's Ride

HENRY WADSWORTH LONGFELLOW

WHY THIS SELECTION?

"Paul Revere's Ride" is an excellent example of narrative poetry, with clearly delineated characters, setting, and plot. Students should find this famous poem about a legendary figure from American history both compelling and entertaining.

ABOUT THIS SELECTION

Student/Teacher's Edition Pages: 136–143

Summary On the evening of April 18, 1775, Paul Revere awaits news about whether British troops are going to attack by land or by sea. Using a lantern signal, Revere's spy tells him the British are arriving by sea. Revere then begins his midnight ride through the towns of Middlesex Country, warning of the British troops' impending arrival. He delivers his message in Medford, Lexington, and Concord, warning the Patriot colonists.

Engaging the Students This poem offers students an opportunity to explore the key idea of legends. Paul Revere's midnight ride to warn the colonists of the impending British attack is legendary—it is part of the larger than life "story" of the American experience. As students read the poem, they can reflect on other legendary figures and narratives in American history.

COMMON CORE STANDARDS FOCUS

- Narrative Poetry
- Paraphrase

LESSON RESOURCES

Plan and Teach

Student Copy Masters

ℹ️ Lesson resources are also available on the **Teacher One Stop DVD-ROM** and online at <u>thinkcentral.com</u>.

PAUL REVERE'S RIDE

Lesson Plan and Resource Guide

Paul Revere's Ride
Poem by Henry Wadsworth Longfellow

Common Core Focus

RL 4 Determine the meaning of words and phrases as they are used in a text. **RL 5** Analyze how the structure of [a] text contributes to its meaning. **RL 10** Read and comprehend poems.

Unless otherwise noted, all resources can be found in the *Resource Manager*.

ⓘ Lesson resources are also available on the **Teacher One Stop DVD-ROM** and online at **thinkcentral.com.** The Student Edition and selected copy masters are available electronically on the ⌀ **Student One Stop DVD-ROM.**

Student/Teacher's Edition Pages	Additional Resources CM = Copy Master T = Transparency
Focus and Motivate	
❑ Big Question p. 136	
❑ Author Biography and Background Information p. 137	❑ ⓘ Literature and Reading Center at **thinkcentral.com**
Teach	
❑ Narrative Poetry p. 137	
❑ Paraphrase p. 137	❑ Paraphrase CM— English p. 177, Spanish p. 178 🄳
Practice and Apply: Guided Practice	
Selection and Teacher Notes ❑ "Paul Revere's Ride," pp. 138–142	❑ ⌀ **Audio Anthology CD** 🄳 ❑ Reading Fluency CM p. 181 ❑ 🧰 **Best Practices Toolkit** ❑ Sequence Chain p. B21, B45 [T] 🄳 ❑ ⓘ Audio Summaries at **thinkcentral.com**

🄳 = Resources for Differentiation

Student/Teacher's Edition Pages	Additional Resources CM = Copy Master T = Transparency
Practice and Apply: After Reading	
❑ Selection Questions p. 143	❑ Reading Check CM p. 179 ❑ Narrative Poetry CM— English p. 175, Spanish p. 176 Ⓓ ❑ Question Support CM p. 180 Ⓓ ❑ Additional Selection Questions p. 170 Ⓓ ❑ Ideas for Extension p. 171 Ⓓ
Assess and Reteach	
Assess	❑ **Diagnostic and Selection Tests** ❑ Selection Tests A, B/C pp. 51–52, 53–54 Ⓓ ❑ ⓘ ThinkCentral Online Assessment ❑ ✐ ExamView Test Generator on the **Teacher One Stop DVD-ROM**

Reteach
❑   Narrative Poetry
❑   Paraphrase
	❑ ⓘ Level Up Online Tutorials on **thinkcentral.com**
	❑ ⓘ Reteaching Worksheets on **thinkcentral.com**
	  ❑ Literature Lesson 5: Elements of Plot
	  ❑ Literature Lesson 17: Narrative vs. Lyric Poetry
	  ❑ Reading Lesson 4: Recognizing Main Idea and Details

Ⓓ = Resources for Differentiation

PAUL REVERE'S RIDE

Use to supplement the
questions on SE page 143.

Additional Selection Questions

Differentiation Use these questions to provide customized practice with
comprehension and critical thinking skills.

Easy

1. **Recall** What does Paul Revere ask his friend to do? (*He asks him to hang out
one lantern if the British are marching by land and two lanterns if they are
approaching by sea.*)

2. **Restate** What is "the night-wind of the Past" (line 125)? (*It is memory, or
history.*)

3. **When does truth become LEGEND?**
Think of another American legend. What does that person have in common with
Paul Revere? (*American legends might include George Washington, Harriet
Tubman, and Rosa Parks, whose accomplishments are seen as larger than life
and who also contributed to the history of the nation.*)

Average

4. **Analyze Symbolism** In what way is the spark in lines 75–80 a symbol that
supports the poet's main idea? (*The literal spark from the horseshoe symbolizes
the news of the beginning of the revolution, which Revere spreads like a fire.
Longfellow uses this image to remind us that Revere's solitary action had
important and wide-ranging consequences.*)

5. **Evaluate Narrative Poetry** How might "Paul Revere's Ride" be different if it
were a short story instead of a narrative poem? (*Students might say that, without
rhythm and rhyme, the tale might be less entertaining.*)

6. **When does truth become LEGEND?**
If Paul Revere had failed in his mission, do you think he would still be an
American legend? Why or why not? (*Students will probably say that he is a
legend only because he was successful—he represents the successful fight for
freedom. Other students may say that Revere would have been legendary for his
bravery either way.*)

Challenging

7. **When does truth become LEGEND?**
"Paul Revere's Ride" includes several references to the past and the future. What
is Longfellow saying about the importance of history? Cite evidence from the
poem to support your answer. (*He is urging future generations, "my children"
[line 1], to remember Paul Revere's ride, especially during dangerous times,
"the hour of darkness and peril and need" [line 127]. He thinks that future
generations can learn valuable lessons from the past.*)

Ideas for Extension

Differentiation These activities provide students with a variety of options for demonstrating understanding of lesson concepts.

EXPLORATIONS AND ACTIVITIES

DRAW CARTOONS: IDENTIFY SEQUENCE OF EVENTS

Review the sequence of events of the poem. Then have students draw a series of cartoons showing what happened on the night of April 18, 1775. Encourage them to include details of setting and dialogue from the poem.

Invite students to display their cartoons and check to see if they have portrayed the correct sequence of events. Discuss any variations in their representation of events.

VENN DIAGRAM: COMPARE AND CONTRAST ELEMENTS OF POETRY

Give students copies of other Longfellow poems, including *The Song of Hiawatha,* "The Village Blacksmith," and "The Wreck of the Hesperus." Ask students to use a Venn diagram to compare and contrast elements in these poems, such as theme, tone, and rhythm, with corresponding elements of "Paul Revere's Ride."

Pre-AP Challenge: Have students prepare dramatic readings of one of these poems.

MEMORIZE POETRY: ANALYZE POETIC STRUCTURE

Tell the class that many students over the years have memorized "Paul Revere's Ride." Discuss strategies that could be used for memorizing it. Point out that within each stanza, the last word in each line rhymes with at least one other line. The rhythm of the poem, though not strictly iambic, is regular, with four stressed syllables in each line. And the story is told in chronological order, which minimizes confusion.

Have students memorize some or all of the poem. You may wish to have each student memorize a stanza and then recite the poem aloud as a group. Encourage students to listen carefully to determine when it is their turn to speak. Remind students to speak clearly and loudly enough for the class to hear.

INQUIRY AND RESEARCH

PAUL REVERE'S REAL RIDE

Explain that Henry Wadsworth Longfellow took some liberties with the factual details of Paul Revere's ride. Several different accounts of the events of the early morning of April 18, 1775, exist, many of which contradict Longfellow's version.

Ask students to research the events of the night of April 18, 1775. Encourage them to look for primary as well as secondary sources to answer the following questions: What role did William Dawes and Dr. Prescott play in the midnight ride? What role did Paul Revere play? Then have students present a report to the class in which they discuss the ways in which the poem reflects or differs from the actual events.

EARLY DAYS OF THE REVOLUTIONARY WAR

Explain that the colonists did not have an official army, but that the colonial militia was able to force the British back to Boston. British casualties in the early battles were high.

Have small groups do library and Internet research to find information about the first days of fighting between the colonists and the British. They might divide the research along the following lines: (1) details of military strategy; (2) comparisons of the training and equipment of the colonial militia and the British army. Then have students share what they have learned and discuss the advantages a "guerrilla army," such as the colonial militia, can have over a larger, more organized military force.

WRITING

EXPLORE GENRE: NARRATIVE POEM

Discuss events in American history that would fit well into the narrative form and that have a heroic main character or characters. Possibilities include the signing of the Declaration of Independence, Lincoln's issuance of the Emancipation Proclamation, Rosa Parks's act of civil disobedience, and the first walk on the moon.

Invite students to choose one of these events and write a narrative poem about the event, imitating the style of "Paul Revere's Ride." Encourage them to read some or all of their poems aloud. Then, as a class, discuss the form and content of the poems.

ANALYZE PERSPECTIVES: SCENE

Ask students to imagine that they and the rest of their family are living in Lexington in 1775 and that they are awakened when Paul Revere rides through their town. What would their first thoughts be? What would they say to each other?

Have students write a dialogue for a family in that situation. They should try to incorporate into the conversation details they have learned about the period and the situation faced by the colonists on the eve of the Revolutionary War. Encourage volunteers to perform their scenes in front of the class.

SUMMARIZE MAIN IDEAS AND DETAILS: BIOGRAPHY

Inform students that Paul Revere was a silversmith and an engraver, and one of colonial America's most talented craftsmen. He became famous for an engraving of the Boston Massacre.

Provide students with biographical information on Paul Revere. Ask them to take notes on details about his craftsmanship and to study examples of his work. Then have them synthesize this information into their own two- or three-paragraph biographical sketch. Suggest that they illustrate the sketch with images of Revere's engravings.

PAUL REVERE'S RIDE

Teacher Notes

Review and Evaluate Outcome
What did I want students to know or be able to do?
How successful was the lesson?

Evaluate Process
What worked?
• Strategies
• Resources
• Differentiation
What did not work? Why not?

Reflect
The next time I teach "Paul Revere's Ride," what will I do differently? Why?

Plan Ahead
What must I do next?

PAUL REVERE'S RIDE

PAUL REVERE'S RIDE

Text Analysis

NARRATIVE POETRY

A narrative poem is a poem that tells a story. Like a short story, a narrative poem has
the following elements:

- a **plot,** or series of events that center on a conflict faced by a main character
- a **setting,** the time and place(s) where the story occurs; setting is usually established in the exposition stage of the plot
- **character(s),** or the individual or individuals who take part in the action

Directions: In the chart, record the story elements in "Paul Revere's Ride."

	"Paul Revere's Ride"
Setting:	
Characters:	
Main Plot Events:	• • • • •

PAUL REVERE'S RIDE

EL PASEO DE PAUL REVERE

Text Analysis

NARRATIVE POETRY

Un poema narrativo es un poema que narra un relato. Como un cuento corto, un poema narrativo tiene los siguientes elementos:

- **trama,** o serie de acontecimientos que se centran en un conflicto al que se enfrenta el personaje principal.
- **escenario,** el tiempo y el (los) lugar(es) donde sucede la historia. El escenario se establece generalmente en la etapa de exposición de la trama.
- **personaje(s),** o el individuo o individuos que toman parte en la acción.

Instrucciones: En la tabla, anota los elementos de la historia de "El paseo de Paul Revere".

	"El paseo de Paul Revere"
Escenario:	
Personajes:	
Acontecimientos de la trama principal:	• • • • •

SPANISH

PAUL REVERE'S RIDE

Reading Skill

PARAPHRASE

Restating complete information in simpler terms is called **paraphrasing.** A good paraphrase includes all of the main ideas and supporting details of the original source and is usually just as long, or longer. Paraphrasing challenging passages can help you better understand them.

> *Original:* Meanwhile his friend through alley and street, Wanders, and watches, with eager ears .

> *Paraphrase:* At the same time, his friend walks through quiet Streets and alleys, looking and listening carefully.

Directions: In the chart, paraphrase the passages listed in the first column.

Line Numbers	Paraphrase
11–14	
42–48	
97–100	
107–110	
113–114	
125–128	

PAUL REVERE'S RIDE

EL PASEO DE PAUL REVERE

Reading Skill

PARAPHRASE

Presentar con otras palabras la información completa en términos simples se le llama **parafrasear.** Una buena paráfrasis incluye todas las ideas principales y detalles de apoyo de la fuente original, y con frecuencia es igualo más larga que el original. Parafrasear pasajes difíciles puede ayudarte a entenderlos mejor.

> *Original:* Entretanto su amigo a través callejones y calles Deambula, y vigila, con oídos ávidos . . .

> *Paráfrasis:* Al mismo tiempo, su amigo camina a través de las calles y los callejones tranquilos, mirando y escuchando cuidadosamente.

Instrucciones: En la tabla, parafrasea los pasajes de la lista de la primera columna.

Líneas	Paráfrasis
11–14	
42–48	
97–100	
107–110	
113–114	
125–128	

SPANISH

PAUL REVERE'S RIDE

Reading Check

Directions: Recall all characters and events in the narrative poem. Then answer each question in sentences or phrases.

1. What does Paul Revere's friend hear as he wanders about the town at night?

_____

_____

_____

2. Why does Paul Revere's friend climb the North Church tower?

_____

_____

_____

3. How does Paul Revere deliver his midnight message?

_____

_____

_____

4. Who receives Paul Revere's message?

_____

_____

_____

5. What effect does Paul Revere's ride have on the events of the next day?

_____

_____

_____

PAUL REVERE'S RIDE

PAUL REVERE'S RIDE

Question Support

TEXT ANALYSIS

For questions 1–3; see page 143 of the Student Edition.

Directions: Answer the questions.

4. Analyze Narrative Poetry Complete the sentences.

In "Paul Revere's Ride," the main conflict is _____

_____

This conflict is resolved _____

_____

5. Understand Paraphrasing Write a paraphrase that describes the purpose of Paul Revere's ride.

_____

_____

_____

6. Analyze Suspense How does Longfellow create suspense, or excitement, in this poem?

_____

_____

_____

7. Evaluate Sensory Details Describe one image from the poem that you find striking.

_____

_____

_____

PAUL REVERE'S RIDE

PAUL REVERE'S RIDE

Reading Fluency

CHORAL READING

By changing the way you read a poem, you can bring out different ideas and meanings. For example, adding stress to a word can give it importance. Changing the rhythm or tone of your voice can create a different mood.

A. Directions: With a small group try three different ways of reading "Paul Revere's Ride," pages 138–142 of the anthology. Then discuss the effect of each reading.

Reading 1: Different Voices

Assign sets of stanzas to different individuals or pairs to read aloud. Have everyone read the last stanza together.

Reading 2: Changing Speed, Volume, and Expression

Read the poem again, changing the inflection as well as how loudly or how fast you read to show the mood of each stanza.

Reading 3: Emphasis

Ask three people to read lines 6–14 of "Paul Revere's Ride" in a manner that stresses the crucial nature of Revere's directions. Decide which interpretation is clearest and most effective.

B. Directions: As a group, write instructions for reading the poems aloud. Have another group use your directions to read the poem to the class.

_____
_____
_____
_____
_____
_____
_____
_____
_____
_____
_____

PAUL REVERE'S RIDE

The Other Riders

WHY THIS SELECTION?

This history article informs students of the facts behind Paul Revere's ride to Concord, exposing some surprising truths about what actually happened and who was involved. Students may wish to discuss some of the ways in which historical events become legends, as is the case with the poem "Paul Revere's Ride."

ABOUT THIS SELECTION

Student/Teacher's Edition Pages: 144–147
Difficulty Level: Challenging
Readability Scores: Lexile: 1260; Fry: 7; Dale-Chall: 8.2

Summary This article tells how William Dawes and Samuel Prescott rode with Paul Revere to inform patriots of an anticipated British military operation in Concord. In fact, Samuel Prescott, not Paul Revere, was the rider who actually delivered the warning to Concord.

COMMON CORE STANDARDS FOCUS

- Take Notes
- Compare and Contrast

LESSON RESOURCES

Plan and Teach

Student Copy Masters

ⓘ Lesson resources are also available on the **Teacher One Stop DVD-ROM** and online at <u>thinkcentral.com</u>.

Lesson Plan and Resource Guide

The Other Riders
History Article

Common Core Focus

RI 1 Cite the evidence that supports an analysis of what the text says explicitly. **RI 9** Analyze a case in which two or more texts provide conflicting information on the same topic and identify where the texts disagree. **W 2** Write explanatory texts.

Unless otherwise noted, all resources can be found in the *Resource Manager*.
ℹ Lesson resources are also available on the **Teacher One Stop DVD-ROM** and online at **thinkcentral.com**. The Student Edition and selected copy masters are available electronically on the 💿 **Student One Stop DVD-ROM.**

Student/Teacher's Edition Pages	Additional Resources CM = Copy Master T = Transparency
Focus and Motivate	
❏ What's the Connection? p. 144	❏ 💼 **Best Practices Toolkit** ❏ Anticipation Guide p. A14 [T]
Teach	
❏ Take Notes p. 144	❏ Take Notes CM—English p. 191, Spanish p. 193 🅓
Practice and Apply: Guided Practice	
Selection and Teacher Notes ❏ "The Other Riders," pp. 145–146	❏ 💿 **Audio Anthology CD** 🅓 ❏ Summary CM—English and Spanish p. 189, Haitian Creole and Vietnamese p. 190 🅓 ❏ 💼 **Best Practices Toolkit** ❏ Whip Around p. B1 🅓 ❏ ℹ Audio Summaries at **thinkcentral.com**
Practice and Apply: After Reading	
❏ Selection Questions p. 147	❏ Reading Check CM p. 195 ❏ Question Support CM p. 196 🅓 ❏ Additional Selection Questions p. 186 🅓
❏ Read for Information: Compare and Contrast p. 147	❏ Compare and Contrast CM—English p. 192, Spanish p. 194 🅓

🅓 = Resources for Differentiation

THE OTHER RIDERS

Student/Teacher's Edition Pages	Additional Resources CM = Copy Master T = Transparency
Assess and Reteach	
Assess	❑ **Diagnostic and Selection Tests** ❑ Selection Tests A, B/C pp. 55–56, 57–58 Ⓓ ❑ ❶ ThinkCentral Online Assessment ❑ ✐ ExamView Test Generator on the **Teacher One Stop DVD-ROM**
Reteach ❑ Take Notes	❑ ❶ Level Up Online Tutorials on **thinkcentral.com** ❑ ❶ Reteaching Worksheets on **thinkcentral.com** ❑ Informational Texts Lesson 1: Text Features

Ⓓ = Resources for Differentiation

THE OTHER RIDERS

Additional Selection Questions

Use to supplement the
questions on SE page 147.

Differentiation Use these questions to provide customized practice with
comprehension and critical thinking skills.

Easy

1. **Recall** Who sent Dawes and Revere on their journey? (*Joseph Warren gave
   them orders to alert Concord.*)
2. **Clarify** Where did Paul Revere and William Dawes meet? (*They met in
   Lexington.*)
3. **Identify Cause and Effect** Why was Prescott able to lose the soldiers
   following him and get to Concord speedily? (*He knew various shortcuts.*)

Average

4. **Take Notes** What facts from the map might you add to your chart under an
   additional subheading called "conclusions"? (*Students might say that they would
   add details about the conclusions of both Revere's and Dawes's journeys.
   Judging by the map, Paul Revere stopped somewhere between Lexington and
   Concord and Dawes returned to Lexington.*)
5. **Evaluate History Articles** How is the information in the article organized?
   Why is this pattern effective? (*The article is organized chronologically, which
   helps readers to understand the sequence of events clearly.*)
6. **Make Inferences** Why did Dawes smuggle gold coins out of Boston?
   (*Knowing that he is a patriot, students will probably infer that he smuggled the
   coins to help other patriots buy ammunition and build up supplies in preparation
   for rebellion against the British.*)
7. **Take Notes** What other type of graphic organizer might have been used to help
   organize notes from this article? (*A sequence chart or outline format might have
   been used.*)

Challenging

8. **Take Notes** How might the notes under each subheading be further organized?
   (*Students might say that they could use bullet points or number the events that
   occurred.*)
9. **Analyze History Articles** One challenge facing a writer is to keep readers
   interested in his or her topic. How does the writer of this article accomplish that
   goal? (*This writer adds personal details, such as Dawes smuggled out gold coins
   as buttons, he was witty and friendly, and Prescott was visiting his girlfriend.
   The writer also includes direct quotations and humorous excerpts from poems.
   The writer's tone is not too formal but sounds as if he or she is telling a story.*)
10. **Make Inferences** Why didn't Paul Revere and William Dawes leave Boston by
    the same route? (*Their departure together might have aroused suspicion. They
    may have had to leave at different times. They might have had different stops to
    make on the way out of the town.*)

Teacher Notes

Review and Evaluate Outcome
What did I want students to know or be able to do?   How successful was the lesson?

Evaluate Process
What worked? • Strategies   • Resources   • Differentiation   What did not work? Why not?

Reflect
The next time I teach "The Other Riders," what will I do differently? Why?

Plan Ahead
What must I do next?

THE OTHER RIDERS

Summary

THE OTHER RIDERS

Setting: Concord, Massacusetts; April 18, 1775

Dr. Joseph Warren asks Paul Revere and William Dawes to warn John Hancock and Samuel Adams about the proposed attack by the British to seize ammunition in Concord. Dawes is able to sneak past British guards.

Continuing on his journey, Dawes meets Paul Revere. They notify Hancock and Adams of the attack. Dawes and Revere set out for Concord together, now joined by Dr. Samuel Prescott. Revere, the leader runs into a British roadblock. Dawes and Prescott are captured. They escape, but Dawes cannot go on because his horse is tired. Prescott warns the town of Concord.

LOS OTROS JINETES

Escenario: Concord, Massachusetts; 18 de abril de 1775

El Dr. Joseph Warren les pide a Paul Revere y a William Dawes que prevengan a John Hancock y a Samuel Adams sobre el ataque planeado por los británicos para apoderarse de las municiones en Concord. Dawes logra escabullirse de los guardias británicos.

Dawes continúa su recorrido y se reúne con Paul Revere. Ellos le avisan a Hancock y a Adams del ataque. Dawes y Revere se van juntos hacia Concord, ahora acompañados por el Dr. Samuel Prescott. Revere, el lider, se topa con una barricada de británicos. Capturan a Dawes y a Prescott. Se escapan, pero Dawes no se puede ir porque su caballo está cansado. Prescott pone en alerta al pueblo de Concord.

Summary

LÒT KAVALYE YO

Espas ak tan: Concord, Massachusetts; 18 avril 1775

Doktè Jozèf Warenn mande Pòl Rivi ak Wilyam Dòwz pou yo avèti Djonn Hannkòk ak Samwèl Adams sou atak Britanik yo gen entansyon fè pou yo sezi tout minisyon ki nan Concord. Dòwz kapab pase an kachèt anba je gad Britanik yo.

Pandan Dòwz ap kontinye vwayaj li, li rankontre Pòl Rivi. Yo fè Hannkòk ak Adams konnen atak la. Dòwz ak Rivi pran wout pou y ale nan Concord ansanm, epi Doktè Samwèl Preskat vin jwenn yo. Rivi, lidè a kouri nan yon baraj wout Britanik yo. Yo kaptire Dòwz ak Preskat. Yo sove, men Dòwz pa ka kontinye paske cheval li a fatige. Preskat avèti vil Concord la.

NHỮNG KỴ MÃ KHÁC

Bối cảnh: Concord, Massacusetts; Ngày 18 tháng 4, 1775

TS. Joseph Warren yêu cầu Paul Revere và William Dawes cảnh báo John Hancock và Samuel Adams về cuộc tấn công đã được đề xuất của Anh nhằm chiếm hữu quân dụng ở Concord. Dawes có thể lên qua lính gác của Anh.

Khi tiếp tục hành trình của mình, Dawes gặp Paul Revere. Họ thông báo cho Hancock và Adams về cuộc tấn công. Dawes và Revere cùng lên đường đi Concord, và bây giờ TS. Samuel Prescott đi với họ. Revere là thủ lĩnh chạy vào hàng rào kiểm soát của Anh. Dawes và Prescott bị bắt. Họ chốn thoát nhưng Dawes không thể đi tiếp vì con ngựa của họ bị mệt. Prescott cảnh báo thị trấn này về Concord.

THE OTHER RIDERS
Skill Focus

TAKE NOTES

When you read an article for social studies or science class, one good way to digest a lot of information is to **take notes.** Writing down important facts and ideas can help you remember them.

Here are some tips for notetaking:

- First, preview the article by looking at its title, subheadings, topic sentences, and graphic aids to determine its topic and main ideas.
- Next, decide how to organize your notes. Can you use the subheadings to create a simple outline or a graphic organizer like the one shown?
- As you take notes, record the main ideas and only the most important facts and details under the appropriate headings. Be sure to include the names, dates, and terms that are necessary for a full understanding of the material.

Directions: In the chart, record notes about "Paul Revere's Ride" and "The Other Riders." An example has been done for you.

from "Paul Revere's Ride"	from "The Other Riders"
	Night of April 18, 1775, a rumor reaches William Dawes that the British are planning to take capture ammunition stores in Concord

THE OTHER RIDERS

THE OTHER RIDERS

Reading for Information

COMPARE AND CONTRAST

When you **compare and contrast,** you identify the ways in which two or more things are alike and different. Then follow these steps:

1. In a chart, identify the main people and events in the poem. Then identify the main people and events in the article.

2. Note the differences between the two accounts in the last column of the chart.

3. In a sentence, make a general statement about the similarities and differences in the accounts. Support your statement with specific examples.

Directions: In the chart, identify the main people and events in the poem and the article. Use the back of this sheet if you need more room to list the events. Record the differences in the two accounts in the last column. Finally, write an original sentence explaining the similarities and differences in the poem and essay.

	From "Paul Revere's Ride"	From "The Other Riders"	Differences
Main Participants			
Main Events			

Sentence: _____

_____

_____

THE OTHER RIDERS

LOS OTROS JINETES
Skill Focus

TAKE NOTES

Cuando lees un artículo para ciencias sociales o para la clase de ciencias, una buena manera de resumir mucha información es **tomar notas.** Escribir hechos e ideas importantes te puede ayudar a recordarlas.

   Aquí hay unos consejos para la toma de notas:.

- Primero, revisa con antelación el artículo observando su título, subtítulos, oraciones del tema y ayudas gráficas para determinar el tema e ideas principales.
- Después, decide cómo organizar tus notas. ¿Puedes usar los subtítulos para crear una reseña simple o un organizador gráfico como el que mostramos?
- Mientras tomas notas, escribe las ideas principales y sólo los hechos y los detalles más importantes bajo los títulos apropiados. Asegúrate de incluir los nombres, fechas y los términos necesarios para una comprensión completa del material.

Instrucciones: En la tabla, escribe notas sobre "el paseo de Paul Revere" y "Los otros jinetes". Sigue el ejemplo.

tomado de "El paseo de Paul Revere"	tomado de "Los otros jinetes"
	La noche del 18 de abril de 1775, el rumor de que los británicos están planeando capturar las tiendas de municiones en Concord llega a oídos de William Dawes.

SPANISH

LOS OTROS JINETES

Reading for Information

COMPARE AND CONTRAST

Cuando **comparas y contrastas,** identificas las maneras en que dos o más cosas se parecen o son diferentes. Ahora sigue los siguientes pasos.

1. En una tabla, identifica a las personas y los acontecimientos más importantes de un poema. Después identifica a las personas y los acontecimientos más importantes del artículo.

2. Anota las diferencias entre las dos narraciones en la última columna de la tabla.

3. En una oración, haz una declaración general sobre las similitudes y diferencias de las narraciones. Apoya tu declaración con ejemplos específicos.

Instrucciones: En la tabla, identifica a las personas y los acontecimientos principales del poema y del artículo. Usa la parte de atrás de esta hoja si necesitas más espacio para escribir los acontecimientos. Registra las diferencias de las dos narraciones en la última columna. Finalmente, escribe una oración original explicando las similitudes y las diferencias del poema y del ensayo.

	Tomado de "El paseo de Paul Revere"	Tomado de "Los otros jinetes"	Diferencias
Participantes principales			
Acontecimientos principales			

Oración: _____

_____

_____

SPANISH

THE OTHER RIDERS
Reading Check

Directions: Recall the events in this history article. Then answer the questions in phrases or sentences.

1. What rumors alarmed the people of Boston on April 18, 1775?

_____

_____

_____

2. What did Joseph Warren order William Dawes and Paul Revere to do?

_____

_____

_____

3. How did Dawes sneak out of Boston?

_____

_____

_____

4. During his ride to Lexington, how did Dawes help spread the word?

_____

_____

_____

5. How did Dawes escape capture?

_____

_____

_____

THE OTHER RIDERS

THE OTHER RIDERS

Question Support

TEXT ANALYSIS

For questions 1–3, see page 147 of the Student Edition.

Directions: Answer the questions.

4. Use Your Notes Write the letters of the five events beside the correct numbers to place them in the order in which they occurred.

1. _____

    A. Prescott warns Concord about the British march.

2. _____

    B. Dawes pulls into the yard of a house and scares off his pursuers.

3. _____

    C. Dawes sneaks into the gates of Boston Neck.

4. _____

    D. Dawes and Revere receive orders from Dr. Warren to ride to inform the leaders of the Provincial Congress of what is going on.

5. _____

    E. A rumor reaches William Dawes that the British are planning to capture ammunition stores in Concord.

5. Understand a History Article Complete the sentence.

One reason "The Other Riders" was written is _____

_____

_____

Essential Course of Study ECOS Lesson at a Glance

Writing Workshop | Personal Narrative

WHAT'S THE CONNECTION?

By writing an personal narrative, students will be able to utilize many of the literary elements and techniques they have studied throughout the unit, including these:

- Stages of plot (exposition, rising action, climax, falling action, resolution)
- Suspense
- Sequence (flashback)
- Foreshadowing
- Conflict
- Personal narrative

In addition, students will have opportunities to incorporate what they have learned in the unit by using a clear order of events, descriptive details, dialogue, appropriate style, sensory language, and varied sentence types. Finally, using the Common Core Traits to develop their own narratives will help students acquire a stronger understanding of plot, conflict, and setting.

ABOUT THE WRITING WORKSHOP

Student/Teacher's Edition Pages: 148–159

The Writing Workshop reinforces the unit focus of narrative structure by supporting students in the writing of a narrative. The workshop provides step-by-step instructions, suggestions, and models for using the writing process.

LESSON RESOURCES

Plan and Teach

Student Copy Masters

ℹ Lesson resources are also available on the **Teacher One Stop DVD-ROM** and online at **thinkcentral.com**.

Lesson Plan and Resource Guide

Writing Workshop

Common Core Focus

W 3a–e Write narratives to develop real or imagined experiences or events using effective technique, relevant descriptive details, and well structured event sequences. **W 4** Produce clear and coherent writing in which the development, organization, and style are appropriate to task, purpose, and audience. **W 5** Develop and strengthen writing as needed by planning, revising, editing, rewriting, or trying a new approach, focusing on how well purpose and audience have been addressed. **W 10** Write routinely over shorter time frames for a range of tasks, purposes, and audiences. **L 1** Demonstrate command of standard English grammar and usage when writing. **L 2a** Use punctuation to indicate a pause or break.

Unless otherwise noted, all resources can be found in the *Resource Manager*. ❶ Lesson resources are also available on the **Teacher One Stop DVD-ROM** and online at **thinkcentral.com**. The Student Edition and selected copy masters are available electronically on the ✏ **Student One Stop DVD-ROM.**

Student/Teacher's Edition Pages	Additional Resources CM = Copy Master T = Transparency
Focus and Motivate	
❑ Write With a Purpose p. 148	❑ ✏ **WriteSmart CD-ROM** ❑ ❶ Writing Center at **thinkcentral.com**
Teach	
❑ Planning/Prewriting pp. 149–150	❑ Planning/Prewriting CM p.201 ❑ Writing Support CM p.208 ❑ ❶ Interactive Graphic Organizers on **WriteSmart CD-ROM**
Practice and Apply: Guided Practice	
❑ Drafting p.151 ❑ Revising, pp. 152–154	❑ Drafting CM p. 202 ❑ Writing Support CM p. 208 🅳 ❑ ❶ Writing Templates on **WriteSmart CD-ROM** and online at **thinkcentral.com** ❑ Revising and Editing 1 CM p. 203 ❑ Ask a Peer Reader CM p. 205 ❑ ✏ **WriteSmart CD-ROM** ❑ ❶ Interactive Revision Lessons on **WriteSmart CD-ROM** and online at **thinkcentral.com** ❑ ❶ **GrammarNotes DVD-ROM** and online at **thinkcentral.com**

🅳 = Resources for Differentiation

Student/Teacher's Edition Pages	Additional Resources CM = Copy Master T = Transparency
	❏ 💼 **Best Practices Toolkit** ❏ Writing Template: Autobiographical or Personal Narrative pp. C16, C18 [T]
Editing and Publishing	
❏ Editing and Publishing p. 155	❏ Revising and Editing 2 CM p. 204 ❏ ❶ **GrammarNotes DVD-ROM** and online at **thinkcentral.com**
Assess and Reteach	
❏ Scoring Rubric p. 156	❏ Scoring Rubric CM p. 206 ❏ ❶ Rubric Generator on **Write*Smart* CD-ROM** and online at **thinkcentral.com** ❏ ❶ Level Up Online Tutorials on **thinkcentral.com** ❏ ❶ Reteaching Worksheets on **thinkcentral.com**
Speaking and Listening	
❏ Presenting an Oral Narrative p. 158	❏ Speaking and Listening CM p. 207

Ⓓ = Resources for Differentiation

WRITING WORKSHOP
Teacher Notes

Review and Evaluate Outcome
What did I want students to learn about writing an personal narrative?
How successful was the lesson?

Evaluate Process
What worked?
• Strategies
• Resources
• Writing Prompts
• Speaking and Listening: Presenting an Oral Narrative
What did not work? Why not?

Reflect
The next time I teach this Writing Workshop, what will I do differently? Why?

Plan Ahead
What must I do next?

WRITING WORKSHOP
Personal Narrative

PLANNING/PREWRITING
A spider map, cluster diagram, or other graphic organizer can help you gather important details about your experience.

Directions: Use the spider map to write down important details about the characters, setting, and action associated with the experience. This information will help you plan your narrative.

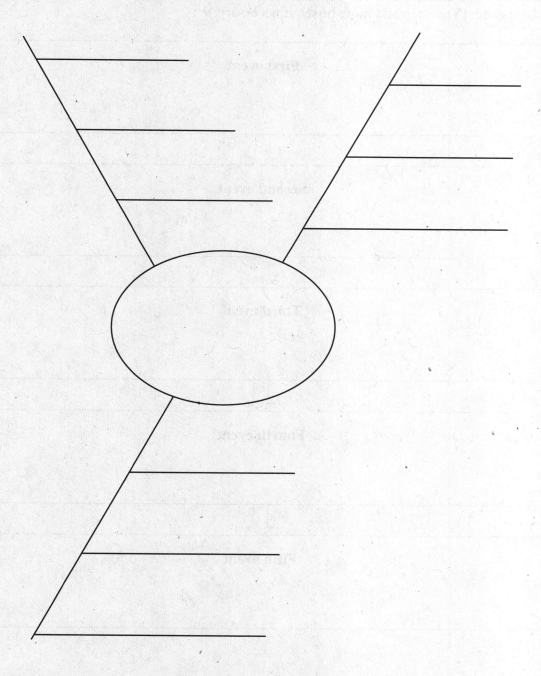

WRITING WORKSHOP

Personal Narrative

DRAFTING

A flow chart can help you organize the narrative's order of events. **Chronological order,** or time order, is usually the clearest way to help readers understand what happened. You can also include a **flashback,** or an event that took place before the start of the narrative.

Directions: Use the flow chart to write down the narrative's events in the order that they happened. (You may add more boxes if necessary.)

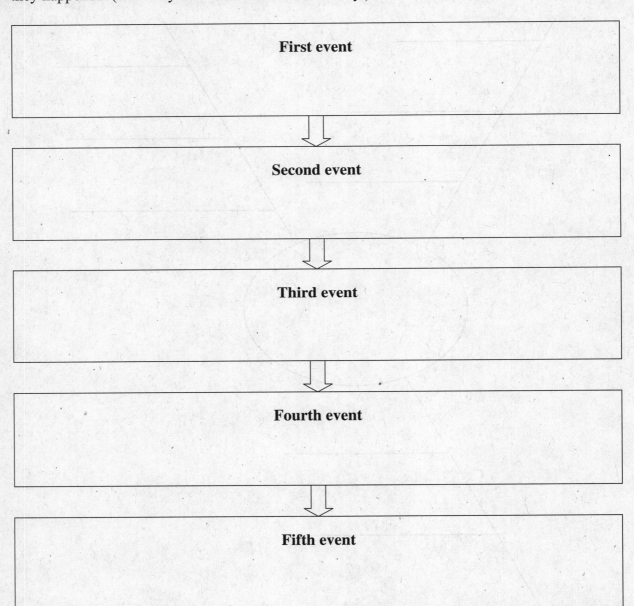

First event

Second event

Third event

Fourth event

Fifth event

WRITING WORKSHOP
Personal Narrative

REVISING AND EDITING 1
The following model is an excerpt from a draft that one student wrote about a meaningful experience in his life.

Directions: Use the following suggestions to revise and edit the excerpt. Mark your changes on this page. Then copy your corrected draft on a separate sheet of paper.
- Use transitions to make the order of events clear.
- Include a variety of sentence types (statements, questions, and exclamations).
- Correct run-on sentences.

A First-Class Smile

Last June, several members of my family took a camping trip together. It began with an early morning flight on a commuter plane. I had never flown before, but I was determined to act cool. My cousin Julio, who flies often, was in the seat next to me. When the flight attendant walks by, I tried my best to look unconcerned. Julio tapped her arm and said, "This plane looks very old." He asked if it was safe.

The attendant said yes, then asked if we had ever flown before. I said nothing. Julio smiled and confessed that he was really nervous about flying. I said, "Why did you tell that woman that you were nervous? It wasn't very cool."

Julio replied, "I do get nervous every time I fly. Flight attendants take really good care of people who are scared but act nice, they want you to come back again."

WRITING WORKSHOP

COPY MASTER

Personal Narrative

REVISING AND EDITING 2

To measure your ability to express ideas clearly and correctly, some tests may ask you to identify errors in grammar and usage and to improve sentences and paragraphs.

Directions: Read each question and select the correct answer.

1. What change, if any, should be made in this sentence?
   I was all excited about the camping trip until I find out that it started with a two-hour flight in a small commuter plane.

   A. Change **excited** to **excitement**
   B. Change **started** to **had started**
   C. Change **find** to **found**
   D. Make no change

2. What is the BEST way to revise this sentence?
   Strapped securely in our seats, the pilot began to taxi down the runway.

   A. Once we were all strapped securely in our seats, the pilot began to taxi down the runway.
   B. Having fastened our seatbelts, the pilot began to taxi down the runway.
   C. Strapped securely in our seats, the pilot began to taxi down the runway.
   D. Make no change

Directions: Read the paragraph and select the correct answer to the question that follows.

3. What is the most effective way to revise sentence 3?
   (1) The trip to the campsite began with a flight in a small commuter plane. (2) In the seat next to me was my cousin Julio. (3) Who flies often. (4) Despite his experience, Julio gets very nervous when he flies. (5) He kept glancing out the window as if he expected a wing to fall off.

   A. Combine sentence 3 with sentence 1.
   B. Add sentence 3 to the end of sentence 2, inserting a comma before *who*.
   C. Place sentence 3 after sentence 4, inserting a comma before *who*.
   D. Make no Change

WRITING WORKSHOP

Personal Narrative

COPY MASTER

ASK A PEER READER

To see whether your autibiographical narrative is interesting and clear, ask a peer reviewer to read it.

Directions: Give your peer reader this sheet. Have him or her record answers to the following questions and then give you suggestions for revision.

1. Does the introduction engage and orient readers and help set the scene?

   _____

   _____

2. Are events in chronological order?

   _____

   _____

3. Are the details describing people, places, and events relevant and precise?

   _____

   _____

4. Does the narrative provide enough background information to engage and orient readers?

   _____

   _____

5. Does the pacing keep events moving smoothly?

   _____

   _____

6. Are there reflections about events in the narrative?

   _____

   _____

7. Does the conclusion reveal why the experience is meaningful?

   _____

   _____

WRITING WORKSHOP

COPY MASTER

Personal Narrative

SCORING RUBRIC

Use the rubric below to evaluate your Personal Narrative. Circle the score that best represents your work. Then use a separate sheet of paper to write a paragraph explaining your score and how you can improve your writing.

SCORE	COMMON CORE TRAITS
6	• **Development** Has an engaging introduction that orients readers; develops events with strong dialogue and description; provides a strong conclusion • **Organization** Establishes a natural and logical sequence of events; uses effective pacing and transitions to convey sequence • **Language** Maintains a clear point of view; uses relevant descriptive details and vivid sensory language; shows a strong command of conventions
5	• **Development** Has an effective introduction; develops events with dialogue and description; provides a conclusion that sums up the narrative • **Organization** Has a logical sequence of events; uses mostly effective pacing and some transitions to signal shifts in time • **Language** Maintains a point of view; includes relevant descriptive details and some sensory language; has a few errors in conventions
4	• **Development** Has an introduction, but doesn't provide context; could use more dialogue or description to develop events; provides an adequate conclusion • **Organization** Has a logical sequence of events but needs more transitions • **Language** Mostly maintains a point of view; needs more descriptive details and sensory language; includes a few distracting errors in conventions
3	• **Development** Has an introduction, but needs more development; needs more dialogue and description; lacks a strong conclusion • **Organization** Has a confusing sequence due to unnecessary events; has a slow pace at times; needs more transitions to convey sequence • **Language** Has some lapses in point of view; lacks effective descriptive details and sensory language; has some major errors in conventions
2	• **Development** Lacks an effective introduction and fails to develop events • **Organization** Includes distracting events; has choppy pacing • **Language** Lacks a clear point of view; mostly lacks details and sensory language; has many errors in conventions
1	• **Development** Has no introduction; lacks descriptive details; ends abruptly • **Organization** Has no transitions and an unclear sequence of events • **Language** Has no clear point of view, no effective details or sensory language; has major conventions errors

WRITING WORKSHOP

Speaking and Listening Workshop

 **Essential Course of Study** ECOS   COPY MASTER

PRESENTING AN ORAL NARRATIVE

Public speaking skills will give you confidence to share your ideas and experiences with others.

Directions: Speakers must carefully choose and supply only those ideas, background information, and details that are essential for a listener. Providing too much information to listeners will make it more difficult for them to understand the key ideas in a speech. In the chart, list essential details and nonessential details from your narrative.

Essential Details	Nonessential Details

WRITING WORKSHOP   COPY MASTER
Writing Support

WRITE SENTENCES WITH TRANSITIONS

Transitions show how things are connected. In your personal narrative, use these words to show how events are connected.

Transitions: Sequence			
Events that happen in sequence		Events that happen at the same time	
then	next	during	as
after	before	meanwhile	at the same time
later	first	while	
the day before	finally	when	

A. Choose the transition words to finish these sentences.

1. _____ the sky became very dark and we came inside.

   _____ it began to rain very hard. We went back outside

   _____ the storm had passed.

2. We had a fire drill _____ we were taking the test. We finished

   the test _____ we came back to our classroom.

USE TRANSITIONS TO DESCRIBE EVENTS IN YOUR NARRATIVE

B. Make a list of events that occur in your narrative.
The events I want to include in my narrative are

_____

_____

C. Use these sentence frames to show the order in which the events in your narrative take place.

1. The first event that happens is _____.

2. The next event that happens is _____.

3. After that, _____ happens.

4. The last event that happens is _____.

Introductory Unit Answer Key

Note Taking
p. I-2

Students' notes will vary. Sample answers are provided.

1. **Elements of fiction:** plot, setting, characters
   Theme: larger messages about life
   Short stories: usually focused on a single event or incident
   Novels: longer works of fiction that weave together different storylines, events, and characters
   Novellas: longer than a short story, but shorter than a novel, with a limited number of characters
2. **Poetry:** a type of literature in which words are chosen and arranged to create certain sounds and meanings
   Poetry is made up of lines and stanzas.
   Sound devices: rhythm and rhyme
3. **Drama:** any work that is written to be performed on stage
   A play is divided into acts and scenes.
   The plot and characters are developed through dialogue.
   Stage directions include descriptions of the setting, characters' movements, and props.
4. Nonfiction is writing that records real-life events.
   Autobiographies and biographies both tell the true story of a person's life.
   Biography: third-person point of view
   Autobiography: first-person point of view
   Essays: short works of nonfiction that focus on a single subject
   Speeches: oral presentation of the ideas, beliefs, or proposals of a speaker
   News articles: report on recent events
   Feature articles: cover human-interest topics
   Other: functional documents
5. **Media:** refers to forms of technology that deliver information
   Types of Media:
   films, TV, Internet, radio, newspapers
   media literate: knowing how to "read" a variety of media messages

Note Taking
p. I-3

Students' notes will vary. Sample answers are provided.
   I.B. Set a purpose for reading; adjust the way you read to suit your purpose
   II.A. recall what you already know about a topic
   II.B. make guesses about what will happen
   II.C. get a clear mental picture of what's happening
   II.D. check your understanding
   II.E. help you read between the lines
   III.A.1. Do any characters remind me of people in my life?
   III.A.2. If I were in this situation, what would I do?

Note Taking
p. I-4

Definition of Academic Vocabulary: the language you use to talk and write about the subject matter you are studying.
Benefits: be successful in school: be successful on tests
Strategies: think about how words are used in other subject areas; use chart to become familiar with words; use activities in textbook to become familiar with words

Note Taking
p. I-5

Students' notes will vary. Sample answers are provided.
1. purpose, format, audience
   The Writing Process
   1. prewriting
   2. drafting
   3. revising and editing
   4. publishing
   Six key traits of effective writing
   • strong, clear topic
   • engaging opening and satisfying conclusion
   • strong sense of individual style
   • precise and colorful language
   • sentences of varied lengths and structures
   • strong grasp of grammar and usage
   (Examples will vary.)

Writing Strategies

1. prewriting, getting feedback from peers, reading
2. freewrite, use graphic organizers, brainstorm, ask questions
3. for specific and honest feedback
4. be respectful of the writer

Unit 1 Answer Key

Unit Opener Copy Masters

Academic Vocabulary
p. 2

1. evident
2. initial
3. affect
4. affect
5. imply

Additional Academic Vocabulary
p. 3

1. establish
2. estimate
3. institute
4. section
5. monitor

Note Taking
p. 7

1. a struggle between opposing forces
2. external, internal

Column 1

External Conflict
This kind of conflict involves a struggle between a character and an outside force
Character vs. Character
Example: Ling confronts Julian over his ridicule of Ling's best friend
Character vs. Force of Nature
Example: Yoni is lost in a snowstorm.
Character vs. Society
Example: Sarah works long hours in a dangerous factory.

Column 2

Internal Conflict
This kind of conflict takes place within a character's own mind.
Character vs. Self

Example: Hannah must decide whether to marry Raj.

Note Taking
p. 8

1. series of events
2. five

1. setting, characters, conflict
2. obstacles/complications, suspense
3. the turning point, at its most intense
4. the outcome of the climax, eases tension, shows how conflict is resolved
5. the final outcome, ties up loose ends

Raymond's Run

Text Analysis
p. 19

Responses will vary. Possible answers are provided

Important Events

1. Squeaky loves running and is fast.
2. Squeaky watches out for her disabled brother Raymond and is fiercely protective of him.
3. Gretchen challenges Squeaky.
4. Squeaky boasts that she will win the May day race.
5. At the race, Squeaky and Gretchen finish at almost the same time.
6. While waiting for the judges' decision, Squeaky realizes that Raymond is a good runner too.
7. Squeaky realizes that there are many things she can do besides running.
8. Squeaky decides to coach Raymond.
9. Squeaky wins the race and Gretchen comes in second, but they smile at each other in mutual respect.

Exposition: 1, 2, 3, 4; Rising Action: 5; Climax: 6; Falling Action: 7; Resolution: 8, 9

Reading Skill
p. 21

Students inferences will vary.

Vocabulary Study
p. 23

A.
1. clutch—Clues: "flexed her fingers," "firmly"
2. crouch—Clues: "low to the ground," "balanced," "push off strongly"
3. liable—Clues: "close," "all of the runners perform well"
4. prodigy—Clue: "talent"
5. relay—Clues: "team," "last runner," "first runners"
6. sidekick—Clue: "followed Gretchen everywhere"

B. Possible meanings:
1. clutch: "grab"
2. crouch: "bend down"
3. liable: "likely"
4. prodigy: "someone who is good at something"
5. relay: "a race run by a team"
6. sidekick: "constant companion"

Vocabulary Practice
p. 24

A.
1. crouch
2. prodigy
3. clutch
4. liable
5. sidekick
6. relay

B.
1. clutch
2. sidekick
3. prodigy
4. relay
5. crouch
6. liable

Vocabulary Strategy
p. 25

A.
1. Indian
2. Japanese
3. French
4. Italian
5. Spanish

B. Answers will vary.

Reading Check
p. 26

1. Raymond has some physical and mental disabilities that make him very childlike. He is subject to "fits of fantasy" and his actions may be unpredictable. Squeaky doesn't seem to mind caring for her brother; she takes her responsibility seriously, and she's very protective of him.
2. She does breathing exercises, and she high-prances along the street to keep her knees strong.
3. Gretchen is a new girl in the neighborhood. She is a good runner, too.
4. Squeaky is very feisty and can hold her own in an argument. She has no tolerance for people who are phony or flighty.
5. At the end of the race, Squeaky no longer thinks that winning is everything. She doesn't have to be the fastest to feel good about herself. Instead, she can find joy in her brother and in possible friendship with Gretchen.

Question Support
p. 27

Text Analysis
4. a, d, e
5. Similarities: same age, serious about running, competitive.
   Differences: Squeaky has to take care of her brother; Gretchen does not. Gretchen has freckles; Squeaky does not. Gretchen has a group of girlfriends; Squeaky is always with her brother.
6. Exposition: Squeaky is introduced. Her love for running and her responsibility for her brother are revealed, Rising Action: Gretchen challenges Squeaky; waiting for the race to begin; waiting to hear who wins, Climax:Squeaky realizes that Raymond is a fast runner, Falling Action and Resolution: Squeaky decides to coach Raymond in running: Squeaky and Gretchen smile at each other in mutual respect.
7. **Part 1**: At the beginning of the story Squeaky loves to run and winning the May Day race is very important to her, **Part 2**: After the race, she realizes that winning isn't everything. She recognizes that Raymond and Gretchen are

also good runners. She also admits that there are other things in life besides running.

8. Squeaky's love for Raymond helps her to put the race into perspective and to better appreciate both him and Gretchen.

Grammar in Context
p. 28

1. (The subject is missing.) I left my books on the table.
2. (The predicate is missing.) The track meet is the last event in the program.
3. (The subject and predicate are missing.) I held my breath during the announcement.
4. (The subject is missing.) I love to run and can't get enough of it.
5. (The subject is missing.) The man with the loudspeaker called my name and then called Gretchen's.

The Ransom of Red Chief

Text Analysis
p. 41

Responses will vary. Possible answers are provided.

Conflict: Kidnappers and boy
Expected Resolution: Boy obeys the men so he can be returned home.
Actual Resolution: Boy terrorizes men into wanting to return boy to his home.
Ironic? Yes.
Conflict: Kidnappers and Mr. Dorset
Expected Resolution: Father pays ransom. Men get money.
Actual Resolution: Men pay ransom demanded by father.
Ironic? Yes

Reading Strategy
p. 43

Responses will vary. Possible answers are provided.

My Prediction: Mr. Dorset will pay the ransom to get his boy back.
Actual Event: Mr. Dorset demands money from the kidnappers to take the boy back.
Correct or Surprised? surprised
My Prediction: The boy will be afraid of his captors.

Actual Event: The boy terrorizes the kidnappers.
Correct or Surprised? surprised
My Prediction: The boy will want to go home.
Actual Event: The boy thinks the whole affair is a fine adventure and has no desire to go home.
Correct or Surprised? surprised
My Prediction: The kidnappers will pay to get rid of the boy.
Actual Event: The kidnappers pay Mr. Dorset to take the boy back.
Correct or Surprised? correct

Vocabulary Study
p. 45

A.

Word in context: collaborate
It is . . .: a verb. It identifies an action.
It is not . . .: descriptive or an object. It is not an adjective, adverb, or noun.
I think it means . . .: work together.
Part of word I recognize: *col*, which means "together"
Related words: collaboration
Examples: doing a school project with someone

B. Accept all reasonable responses. Examples relating to first boldfaced word: Two heads are better than one. When two or more people **collaborate**, they may be able to anticipate and plan for the unexpected more efficiently.

Vocabulary Practice
p. 46

A.

1. collaborate
2. commend
3. diatribe
4. proposition
5. provisions
6. impudent
7. ransom
8. comply

B.

1. diatribe
2. impudent
3. commend
4. comply

Vocabulary Strategy

p. 47

A.

1. compatible
2. conjecture
3. composure
4. confide
5. multimedia
6. multipurpose
7. multicultural
8. multilingual

Reading Check

p. 48

1. The boy throws a brick when Bill offers him candy and a ride.
2. Hyperactive, creative, imaginative, mischievous, mean, a bully.
3. He thinks it's like a camping trip. He enjoys it because he gets to do things he can't do at home.
4. Red Chief is really in charge because the kidnappers are both afraid of what he may do next.
5. He knows that his son is impossible and must be driving the kidnappers crazy.

Question Support

p. 49

Text Analysis

4. The boy would want to stay with the kidnappers.
   The father did not want the son back.
   No one seemed worried about the boy.
   The kidnappers would be so eager to get rid of the boy that they would be willing to pay the father to take him back.
5. Outcome **d** is ironic because you would expect the boy to be threatened or abused by the kidnappers and instead it is the kidnappers who are threatened and abused by the boy. It is just the opposite of what you expect, so the outcome is ironic.
6. **Part 1**: Sam uses big words (many of which he uses incorrectly) in order to make himself sound important, **Part 2**: Most students will say they don't think Bill and Sam have been successful in their previous schemes because they do not have much money (only $600

between the two of them) and they did not study the people involved to devise a kidnap plan that would actually work.

Grammar in Context

p. 50

1. They thought the boy would be afraid, but he actually liked being kidnapped.
2. The boy threw rocks at them. He was more trouble than he was worth.
3. Bill was afraid of being left alone with the boy. He wasn't sure what the boy might do.
4. They thought the boy's father would pay them a ransom, but it turned out that they were the ones who had to pay.
5. The crooks ran away from the boy's house as fast as they could, because they were afraid the boy would run after them.

Clean Sweep

Text Analysis

p. 63

Responses will vary. Possible answers are provided.

Row 1
   External Conflicts: Katie forced to balance school work and cleaning
   Internal Conflicts: Katie misses him and regrets not making him breakfast
   Katie resents him for not leaving enough money

Row 2
   Event: Mrs. Leonardo's family deserts her
   External Conflicts: Mrs. Leonardo refuses to contact family
   Internal Conflicts: Mrs. Leonardo feels she has been taken advantage of

Row 3
   Event: Mrs. Leonardo hires Katie to clean out her attic
   External Conflicts: Mrs. Leonardo vs. Katie over what to keep and what to throw away

Row 4
   Event: Mrs. Leonardo finds an old book in the trunk
   External Conflicts: Mrs. Leonardo vs. Katie over whether or not to call her sister
   Internal Conflicts: Mrs. Leonardo regrets not having given Helen the book she asked for

Reading Skill
p. 65

Students' responses will vary. Sample answers are given.

Katie's father dies.

Katie's mother forms Clean Sweep.

Katie goes to clean out Mrs. Leonardo's attic.

Katie suggests that some things should be thrown away.

Mrs. Leonardo refuses to throw anything away,

Mrs. Leonardo finds a book of bedtime stories that her sister Helen had asked for.

Katie suggests that Mrs. Leonardo call her sister to explain about the book.

Mrs. Leonardo prepares a special meal for her sister.

Katie remembers the book her dad read to them and realizes how important that book is to her.

Vocabulary Study
p. 67

A.
1. aberration—Clues: "decision to help," "usually avoids"; Possible meaning: "unusual action"
2. dingy—Clues: "fingerprints," "stacks of yellowing newspapers"; Possible meaning: "grubby"
3. miniscule—Clues: "chip," "sift through vacuum cleaner bag"; Possible meaning: "small"
4. propriety—Clues: "trust," "act"; Possible meaning: "appropriateness"
5. turmoil—Clue: "or"; Possible meaning: "uncertainty"
6. vile—Clues: "mold," "odor"; Possible meaning: "disgusting"

B.
1. aberration, propriety, vile: An act that is different from someone's usual behavior is an aberration. Propriety refers to proper conduct or behavior. Someone's behavior might be evil or vile.
2. dingy, miniscule, turmoil: The appearance of a place or even person might be described as dingy, meaning dirty or unkempt. An object might be very small or miniscule. A physical location might be in a state of confusion or turmoil, or someone's emotions or thoughts might be described in this way.

3. dingy, vile: Dingy has negative meanings, including dirty and discolored. Vile means unpleasant, also negative in its denotation and connotation.

Vocabulary Practice
p. 68

A.
1. aberration
2. minuscule
3. dingy
4. vileness
5. propriety
6. turmoil

B.
7. d
8. a
9. b
10. b
11. b
12. a

Vocabulary Strategy
p. 69

A.
1. possible + -ity; condition of being possible
2. indicate + -tion; act of indicating
3. ready + -ness; state of being ready
4. persist + -ence; quality of being persistent

B.
1. meditation
2. scarcity
3. independence
4. appointment

Reading Check
p. 70

1. They clean houses.
2. Katie dislikes Mrs. Leonardo and thinks that she is mean.
3. He has died of a heart attack.
4. The stories in the book were her sister's best memories of childhood.
5. Mrs. Leonardo is preparing for a visit from her sister, who is coming to have dinner with her.

Question Support
p. 71

Text Analysis

4. c. Her father died suddenly, e. She was afraid they would lose their house, f. She regrets not making her father breakfast.

5.

Row 1

Conflict: misses her father terribly
Resolution: going through his books and papers helps her feel closer to him

Row 2

Conflict: fears they will lose their house
Resolution: helps her mother with cleaning service and earns enough money to pay bills

6. Mrs. Leonardo realized that she was wrong about the book, and perhaps her alienation from the rest of her family is the result of similar misunderstandings.

7. **Conflict:** They have lost contact because of an argument over a book. Her sister asked for the book; Mrs. Leonardo thought she had given it to her sister.

   Resolution: Mrs. Leonardo finds the book and calls her sister to invite her to dinner.

8. Most students will say that he is a hypochondriac because he claims to have tennis elbow, but doesn't play tennis or because he seems to be sick only when he is supposed to be helping Katie clean. Some students may say he is not a hypochondriac because being allergic to dust can be a serious problem for someone who has to clean out attics and basements.

Grammar in Context
p. 72

Responses will vary.

The Tell-Tale Heart

Text Analysis

p. 85

Rank: 4
Lines 1–78
Techniques:
   1. Narrator's insistence on his sanity
   2. Repetition of actions

Rank: 2
Lines 79–111
Techniques:
   1. Description of heart beating louder and louder
   2. Description of cover up

Rank: 3
Lines 112–133
Techniques:
   1. Narrator's confidence that he won't get caught
   2. Description of narrator's bodily discomfort

Rank: 4
Lines 134–152
Techniques:
   1. Short sentences with exclamation points
   2. Building of tension about being caught

Reading Skill
p. 87

Responses will vary. Possible answers are provided.

Column 1

Makes Me Suspicious: The narrator is planning to murder an old man because he has an evil eye.
The narrator hears the beating of the old man's heart; it gets louder and louder as the story progresses.
The narrator believes that he is too clever to be caught for the murder of the old man.
The narrator keeps insisting that he is not mad.
The narrator commits murder, cuts up the body, and hides it.

Column 2

Makes Me Trust Him:
It appears that he is the old man's caretaker or a relative.
The narrator says he loved the old man and did not want his money.

Vocabulary Study
p. 89

Responses will vary. Sample responses are given.

A.

1. acute: well-developed
2. audacity: daring

3. conceived: thought
4. crevice: crack
5. derision: mockery
6. hypocritical: false
7. Stealthily: secretly
8. stifled: muffled
9. vex: bothered
10. vehemently: passionately

Vocabulary Practice
p. 90

A.
1. vehemently
2. acute
3. crevice
4. stealthily
5. derision
6. hypocritical
7. vex
8. conceived
9. stifled
10. audacity

B.
1. e
2. c
3. a
4. b
5. d

Vocabulary Strategy
p. 91

Answer will cary. Sample answers are given.
1. The **deserted** house has not been lived in for over ten years.
2. The wealthy businessman gave an **insignificant** sum to the charity even though he was able to donate much more.
3. It is **certain** that the runner who trained professionally for a long time will win the race.
4. The students **dispersed** quickly when the assembly was over.
5. It is **likely** that Jan will win the election for class president.
6. It is **unavoidable** that I will have to take algebra and geometry in order to graduate.

Reading Check
p. 92

1. I feel the narrator really is mad, and he knows he is. He thinks that is he tells us he is not; maybe we will believe him and it may just come true.
2. He was waiting for the eye to open because that was the thing he hated and wanted to kill. When the eye was closed, he couldn't feel the anger he needed to kill the old man.
3. The police could not hear the heart beating because the man was dead. The narrator heard it only in his mind, because he knew he had committed a crime.
4. The narrator really confessed because he thought he would get caught anyway, and he knew he needed help. It might be his only chance or someone to cure his insanity.
5. He was most certainly mad. For someone to commit murder, cut up and hide the body, and hear the dead heart beating, he would definitely have to be insane.

Question Support
p. 93

Text Analysis
4. The narrator is most likely the caretaker or caregiver of the old man. There is a possibility that the narrator may be a relative of the old man.
5. Describing a character's anxiety or fear is the most effective technique that Poe used for creating suspense because having the narrator constantly claim that he is sane is an excellent method for creating suspense.

Relating vivid descriptions of dramatic sights and sounds is the most effective technique that Poe used for creating suspense because, for example, hearing the heartbeat get louder and louder increases the suspense.

Repeating words, phrases, or characters' actions is the most effective technique that Poe used for creating suspense because this is an excellent way of building suspense. For example, over seven days, the narrator opens the old man's door, and shines a light in the eye of the old man. Then, in the morning, he asks the old man about his night's sleep. The suspense builds because each time he could commit the murder or get caught.

6. The narrator in "The Tell-Tale Heart" is reliable because he is honest about what he feels and what he has done.

The narrator in "The Tell-Tale Heart" is not reliable because it is difficult to believe what he says. He insists that he is sane, but he murders the old man for an insane reason.

7. The narrator keeps saying that he is sane, but the reader knows that he is crazy. For the reader, this knowledge creates a feeling of tension, or suspense, because the more the narrator insists that he is sane, the more obvious it is that he is about to do something completely irrational.

The Hitchhiker

Text Analysis
p. 105

Responses will vary. Possible answers are provided.

Row 1

Foreshadowing: Mother says I wish you weren't driving; don't pick up any strangers on the road.

Events that were foreshadowed: A hitchhiker causes Adams to nearly have an accident.

Row 2

Foreshadowing: Adams sees the hitchhiker twice in a very short time.

Events that were foreshadowed: He will see the hitchhiker again.

Row 3

Foreshadowing: The mechanic says hitchhikers would be a sight for sore eyes; no one hitchhikes on the road especially during that season.

Events that were foreshadowed: The next time Adams sees the hitchhiker, the figure calls to him.

Row 4

Foreshadowing: Adams gets stuck on the train tracks when he tries to run the hitchhiker down.

Events that were foreshadowed: The hitchhiker just keeps coming back.

Row 5

Foreshadowing: The girl can't see the hitchhiker even though Adams sees him clearly.

Events that were foreshadowed: The girl thinks Adams is crazy and incoherent and leaves his car.

Row 6

Foreshadowing: Adams thinks that if he calls his mother, he will be all right.

Events that were foreshadowed: Something—a Serious illness—has happened to his mother.

Reading Strategy
p. 107

Without the sound effects and stage directions, I would not know about the car veering and skidding, and eventually going into the barbed wire fence. I would not know that the girl screamed, slapped Adams, and opened the car door in order to escape.

Vocabulary Study
p. 109

A.

1. assurance—Clues: "solemn," "drive safely"
2. lark—Clue: "looking forward to it"
3. monotony—Clues: "miles and miles of flat highway," "interrupted"
4. sinister—Clues: "threatening," "fear"
5. junction—Clues: "railroad," "across the tracks"

B.

Possible meanings:
1. assurance: "promise"
2. lark: "adventure"
3. monotony: "sameness"
4. sinister: "evil"
5. junction: "place where two things meet"

Reading Check
p. 110

1. Ronald Adams and his mother are close. She is a reluctant to have him leave on his journey; he calls her when he needs reassurance and help.
2. He is in "excellent spirits". He thinks it will be a "lark".

3. The man is thin and nondescript, a cap is pulled over his eyes, and there are spots of rain on his shoulders. He is carrying a cheap overnight bag. Adams describes him as "drab as a mud fence".

4. He has frightened her by talking about a hitchhiker that she can't see and by driving erratically and dangerously in his attempt to kill the imaginary man.

5. Ronald Adams is seeing the hitchhiker everywhere. Unless he drives eighty-five miles an hour, he sees the figure every other mile, flitting in front of him, no matter what the terrain of the landscape is.

Question Support
p. 111

Text Analysis

4. The relationship between Adams and his mother can best be described as close. Adams's mother is concerned about his driving too fast and falling asleep at the wheel. She also reminds him not to pick up any hitchhikers. She is crying before he leaves on his trip.

5. In this radio play, the most effective use of foreshadowing in increasing the suspense is when the mechanic says he never saw anyone hitchhiking on the road—especially during the time of year in which the play is set.

6. If sound effects and stage directions were taken out of the play, listeners would not fully understand what was happening. For example, they would not hear the sound of the car crashing or the railroad-crossing signal.

7. In the radio play, the hitchhiker represents death or the angel of death. He appears to have some supernatural power since he can travel faster than Adams's car. He is also described as being quite ordinary.

8. One similarity is that they both have suspenseful plots.
One difference is that "The Tell-Tale Heart" takes place indoors, in one location, over the course of one night. *The Hitchhiker* takes place over the course of several days and in several different states.

Grammar in Context
p. 112

1. No one in his or her right mind would want to get a ride from Adams

2. Everybody knows that he or she shouldn't pick up hitchhikers.

3. Anyone with common sense should realize that he or she would be putting himself in danger.

4. Nobody could ever convince me that he or she had seen this man on the side of the road.

5. If anyone ever told me that this experience had happened to him or her, I wouldn't believe it.

Hoot
Text Analysis
p. 114

Responses will vary. Possible answers are provided.

Crime or unexplained Event: He wasn't wearing any shoes and there was not a trace of which school he attended.
Cues and/or Motives: The kid didn't look big enough for high school.
He wasn't wearing shoes.
He was running like crazy.
The next day, from the bus, Roy didn't see the shoeless boy. This happened for the next two days.
Suspense: Roy sees the boy from the bus.
Dana chokes Roy.
Roy disembarks suddenly from the bus, and chases the boy.
Plot Twist: Roy is hit by a golf ball while pursuing the boy across a golf course.
The golfers thought Roy was dead, but he was just very sleepy.

Media Study
Viewing Guide
p. 121

Responses will vary. Possible answers are provided.

Carmen's dad is very important to Carmen.
Carmen is both shocked and troubled by the news.
Carmen longs for a closer connection with her dad.

Close Viewing
p. 122

Responses will vary. Possible answers are provided.

Row 1, Column 2: Carmen is eager to show off her good grades; she is anxious for her dad's approval.

Row 1, Column 3: It shows how much Carmen cares about her father's opinion, she wants to please him.

Row 2, Column 2: Carmen is confused about the woman's identity.

Row 2, Column 3: Carmen thought she was going to spend the whole summer with just her dad; she does not like the idea of another woman spoiling her plans.

Row 3, Column 2: Carmen is shocked and hurt; she does not understand why her father didn't tell her beforehand that he was getting married.

Row 3, Column 3: Now that Carmen's dad is engaged to a woman with her own kids, Carmen feels like an outsider.

My First Free Summer
Text Analysis
p. 135

Responses will vary. Possible answers are provided.

Personal Experiences: "I never had summer—I had summer school." (line 1)

Personal Experiences: "In fifth grade, I vowed I would get interested in fractions, the presidents of the United States, Mesopotamia; I would learn my English." (lines 3–4)

Historical Events: ". . . my father, who was involved in an underground plot, my mother knew that *los americanos* had promised to help bring democracy to the island." (lines 8–10)

Personal Experiences: "Every June, when my prospects looked iffy, Mami and I met with the principal. I squirmed in my seat while they arranged for my special summer lessons." (lines 24–26)

Historical Events: "The plot had unraveled. Every day there were massive arrests. The United States had closed its embassy and was advising Americans to return home." (lines 54–56)

Personal Experiences: The summer of 1960 began in bliss: I did not have to go to summer school! Attitude much improved. Her English progressing nicely . . ." (lines 48–49)

Historical Events: "Every night black Volkswagens blocked our driveway and stayed there until morning. 'Secret police,' my older sister said." (lines 57–59)

Personal Experiences: "Our papers and tickets came! We're leaving for the United States." (lines 68–69)

Historical Events: ". . . a cat-and-mouse game the dictator liked to play." (lines 85–86)

Personal Experiences: I knew that ours was not a trip, but an escape. We had to get to the United States." (lines 93–94)

Reading Skill
p. 137

Cause: political struggles

Effect: The secret police stand watch in their driveway each night.

Effect: The dictator's government could arrest the family.

Effect: Her father is involved in an underground organization hoping to overthrow the dictator, with the help of Americans.

Vocabulary Study
p. 139

1. contradiction—Predicted Meaning: "different idea or opinion"; Meaning in Selection: "a denial; an expression that is opposite"
2. interrogation—Predicted Meaning: "questioning; grilling"; Meaning in Selection: "a formal questioning"
3. replete—Predicted Meaning: "full"; Meaning in Selection: "abundantly supplied"
4. summon—Predicted Meaning: "ask"; Meaning in Selection: "send for; call"
5. unravel—Predicted Meaning: "fall apart"; Meaning in Selection: "to undo; come apart"

Vocabulary Practice
p. 140

A.
1. replete
2. interrogation
3. unravel

4. contradiction
5. summon

B.

6. undo
7. lavish
8. call
9. denial
10. questioning

C. Responses will vary. Accept paragraphs that accurately use at least two of the vocabulary words.

Vocabulary Strategy
p. 141

A.

1. jurisdiction
2. dedicate
3. indictment
4. edict
5. abdicate
6. contradict
7. benediction
8. indicate

B. Sentences will vary. Accept sentences that accurately use any four vocabulary words.

Reading Check
p. 142

1. to learn English, the language of the nation she thought would liberate the Dominican Republic from a repressive dictatorship
2. They had more holidays from school, marched in parades, visited the palace, and had their pictures in the paper.
3. She did not want to attend summer school.
4. They were not taking a trip but making an escape to the United States.
5. She feared that he would not let them enter the United States and that they would have to go back to the Dominican Republic.

Question Support
p. 143

Text Analysis

3. "Free" refers to her first free summer not having to attend summer school. It also refers to being free and escaping the tyranny of her homeland once she arrives in the United States.
4. One way in which Julia Alvarez changes from the beginning of the story to the end is that she

comes to the realization about the dangers of tyranny in the Dominican Republic.
5. One detail in which you can see that this selection is written by an adult is when she is at the airport, ready to leave for the United States, and says, "This had happened before, a cat-and-mouse game the dictator liked to play."
6. One effect that the political struggle had on Alvarez is the police could, at any time, arrest the family due to the father's role in the underground plot to overthrow the dictator.

The Great Rat Hunt
Text Analysis
p. 155

Responses will vary. Possible answers are provided.

Conflict: Laurence feels that his father doesn't like or accept him.
Event: Rat appears.
Event: Rat hunt.
Event: Laurence's father tells him about his past.
Resolution: Laurence feels accepted by his father and better about himself.

Reading Skill
p. 157

Father sets out traps.
He tries poison pellets.
He calls exterminator.
Exterminator fumigates the store.

Father borrows rifle.
The narrator and his father go upstairs to the apartment.
They wait for the rat to appear.

The rat charges at the pair.
The narrator and his father run from the apartment.
The narrator's mother makes fun of the pair.

Vocabulary Study
p. 159

A. Possible meanings:
1. barricade: block
2. brusquely: quickly
3. improvised: invented

4. ineptitude: lack of ability
5. perpetual: constant
6. rationalize: justify
7. ravage: destroy
8. reserve: restraint
9. vigilant: aware
10. wince: flinch

Vocabulary Practice
p. 160

A.
1. ravage
2. improvised
3. brusquely
4. reserve
5. wince
6. perpetual
7. rationalize
8. ineptitude
9. barricade
10. vigilant

B.
1. d
2. c
3. b
4. e
5. a

Vocabulary Strategy
p. 161

Responses will vary.
1. extreme
2. messy
3. inspire
4. take over
5. natural attraction

Reading Check
p. 162

1. He feels left out; he feels like a failure; he feels that he has let his father down. He can't play sports because he has asthma.
2. Yep interprets his father's silence as disappointment or impatience. He takes the silence as personal criticism.
3. He wants to win his father's approval. He wants to seem as brave as he thinks his brother will be.

4. He and his father have been working together as partners. His father has shown he trusts Yep. He seems to enjoy Yep's company.
5. Yep's father says that Yep will find another activity that he's good at. Yep learns that his father is not disappointed in him, and that he is not a failure just because he's not good at sports.

Question Support
p. 163

Text Analysis

4. The event that takes place right before Father runs out of the apartment is the rat charging at Yep and his father.
5. Answers will vary. One conflict that takes place during the memoir is that Laurence feels that his father doesn't like or accept him. The events that lead to the resolution are: (1) the rat appears; (2) the rat hunt takes place; (3) Eddy refuses to hunt the rat; (4) Laurence's father tells him about his past. His father shows acceptance of Laurence. The resolution is that Laurence feels better about himself.
6. Yep agrees to help his father capture the rat because he wants to gain his father's respect. He is also very much intrigued by the rifle.
7. At the beginning of the memoir, Yep feels like an outsider who doesn't belong in the family because asthma prevents him from playing sports.
At the end of the memoir, Yep learns that his father is not perfect, and he does not expect his two sons to be either. Yep's feelings of alienation disappear.
8. "Our" refers to Yep and his father. Yep knows that his father values the experience they have shared in hunting the rat.

Grammar in Context
p. 164

1. had studied
2. felt
3. had searched
4. practices
5. realized

Paul Revere's Ride

Text Analysis
p. 175

Setting: April 18, 1775
Middlesex County, Massachusetts
Characters: Paul Revere
His Friend
The British
Main Plot Events:

- Paul Revere tells his friend to put up one (if by land) or two (if by sea) lantern(s) in the belfry of the Old North Church as a signal of British troop movements.
- The Somerset (a British warship) rows quietly onto the shore.
- His friend hears the British and climbs into the belfry to signal.
- Paul Revere sees the signal and takes off on his horse to warm the citizen army in the country.
- The American troops fought bravely and the British fled.

Reading Skill
p. 177

Responses will vary. Possible answers are provided.

Row 1
I'll wait on the other side of the river, ready to ride out and warn everyone in the countryside to get up and arm themselves.

Row 2
Beneath him lay a cemetery. It was so quiet that he could hear the wind, which was like a night guard, whispering, "All is well!"

Row 3
The windows of the meeting house seemed to stare at him with horror, as if they knew about the bloodshed that would happen later.

Row 4
The man who would be the first to die in battle was safe in his bed right now.

Row 5
How the farmers, hiding behind fences and walls, returned each shot that the British fired.

Row 6
If we are ever again in great danger, the proud history of Revere's message will once again rouse people to action.

Reading Check
p. 179

1. He hears the British soldiers marching down to their boats.
2. He climbs the tower to signal with lanterns that the British are on their way by sea.
3. Paul Revere rides on horseback, calling out a warning and knocking on doors.
4. the villagers and farmers who live throughout the county.
5. The farmers are armed and ready for the British soldiers' attack.

Question Support
p. 180

Text Analysis

4. **Part 1**: the British soldiers' march against the rebel leaders, **Part 2**: when the British turned and ran away from the Americans.
5. Paul Revere hoped to warn the people of the Middlesex villages and farms that the British army was coming so they could stop them.
6. Long fellow creates suspense in this poem by the repetition of time of the village clock.
7. The image of the pigeons being startled in the church tower is striking.

The Other Riders

Skill Focus
p. 191

Responses will vary.

Reading for Information
p. 192

From "Paul Revere's Ride"
Main Participants:
Paul Revere
His Friend
The British

Main Events:
Paul Revere tells his friend to put up one (if by land) or two (if by sea) lantern(s) in the belfry of the Old North Church as a signal for when the British approach.
The Somerset (a British warship) rows quietly onto the shore.
Paul Revere sees the signal and takes off on his horse to warm the citizen army in the country.

The American troops fought bravely and the British fled.

From "The Other Riders"
Main Participants:
William Dawes
Samuel Prescott
Joseph Warren

Main Events:
Dawes tells Paul Revere; both get orders from Dr. Joseph Warren to ride to inform the leaders of the Provincial Congress of what's going on.
Dawes reaches the gate of Boston Neck. He knows how to sneak in and out of the city. He also befriends many British guards. When the gate opens, Dawes sneaks in with some British soldiers.
Travelling west, Dawes alerts more riders, and they get others to join them.
Dawes catches up with Revere in Lexington, alerting Hancock and Adams. Dawes and Revere then go to Concord.
Dr. Samuel Prescott joins them.

Differences: One is a poem; the other is an article. The article focuses on William Dawes and Samuel Prescott, two lesser-celebrated participants in Paul Revere's ride. The article is factual; the poem uses figurative language.

Sentence: The poem celebrates the role of Paul Revere is warning of a British attack, while the article informs readers of the fact that others spread the warning as well.

Reading Check
p. 195

1. rumors that the British were planning to seize ammunition in the town of Concord the next day
2. to ride to the leaders of the Provincial Congress and inform them of the planned British march
3. He had earlier befriended the British guards. One of his friends was on duty, so Dawes slipped out when the guard opened the gate for some British soldiers.
4. He alerted riders from neighboring towns of the planned British march.

5. He pretended to meet with others who could surround the British soldiers who were chasing him.

Question Support
p. 196

Text Analysis
4.
   1. E
   2. D
   3. C
   4. B
   5. A
5. to clear misconceptions about Paul Revere's ride

Writing Workshop
Revising and Editing 1
p. 203

A First-Class Smile

Last June, several members of my family took a camping trip together. It began with an early morning flight on a commuter plane. I had never flown before, but I was determined to act cool. My cousin Julio, who flies often, was in the seat next to
                                    walked
me. When the flight attendant ~~walks~~ by, I tried my best to look unconcerned. Julio tapped her arm and said, "This plane looks
            "Are you sure it's safe?"
very old. ~~He asked if it was safe.~~

The attendant said yes and then asked if we had ever flown
                        but
before. I said nothing. Julio smiled and confessed that he was
                After the attendant left,
really nervous about flying. I said, "Why did you tell that woman that you were nervous? It wasn't very cool."

Julio replied, "I do get nervous every time I fly. Flight attendants take really good care of people who are scared but act nice. They want you to come back again."

Revising and Editing 2
p. 204

1. C
2. A
3. B

Writing Support
p. 208

A.

1. First, Then or Next, after
2. while, after

B. Answers will vary depending on students' personal narratives.

C. Students' sentences will vary, but events should reflect a logical order using the transitions correctly.